HOOSIERS and Scrubby Dutch:
★ St. Louis's South Side ★

★ By Jim Merkel ★

REEDY PRESS

Reedy Press
PO Box 5131
St. Louis, MO 63139, USA

Library of Congress Control Number: 2014946138
ISBN: 978-1-935806-84-4

Please visit our website at www.reedypress.com.

Design by Jill Halpin

Printed in the United States of America
14 15 16 17 18   5 4 3 2 1

Photo Credits:
(Unless noted below, all photos are from the author or publisher.)
Carondelet Historical Society: xii, 38–40, 28–29 (Ironclads), 72–73, 155
Slim Cox: 47
Dogtown Historical Society archives: 191
Library of Congress: 35, 76, 162
Martin Duggan: 9
Mickey McTague: 49
Bruce Marren: 42, 43
National Weather Service: 169
Don Roussin: 170, 173
Jim Shrewsbury: 65
Sinclair Ford: 52
Steve Mizerany: 55
Strosnider family: 97

CONTENTS

PLACES   77

EVENTS   163

UNUSUAL, UNIQUE, OR JUST PLAIN ODD   197

PREFACE

Without Jeff Tobin, my life would be poorer. Jeff was one of my editors at the old *South Side* and *South County Journals*. Early in 2008, he called me into his office and issued a directive: write a weekly column with the name "This Week in South Side History." From that meeting came stories about everything from the Great St. Louis Bank Robbery to the first cow that flew in an airplane. People loved it, and by the middle of 2009 I had enough to fill a book. So I approached Josh Stevens at Reedy Press with an idea to publish those columns in a book. Over coffee, we decided that a better idea was a fresh book of bite-sized stories about the South Side, some I'd written about before and some new.

I ventured forth with pen, notepad, recorder, and camera to capture the essence of the South Side. I stood with my wife next to a stop sign at Fyler and Macklind Avenues to count how many make a grinding stop and how many tap their brakes lightly and then go. I investigated the Frog of Cherokee Street and the strange case of a street that dead-ended and then started up again several feet lower. Anheuser-Busch caught my attention, as did Falstaff and the exorcism that was the basis for the movie *The Exorcist.* For those who haven't heard, it happened right here, at Alexian Brothers Hospital.

I talked to aged women who remembered scrubbing down porches, and surveyed a couple of dozen South Siders about the meaning of the word "hoosier." The most memorable was the man who groused at me, "You callin' me a @*$%@*#$%@ hoosier?" Fortunately, I could withdraw to Ted Drewes, buy my hot fudge concrete and flip it over with the confidence the concoction wouldn't fall out onto the ground. It did. I could have complained about false advertising, but instead went back to buy another one. Refreshed, I sought out more of the people who made the South Side what it is. Sitting in a Chippewa Street furniture store crammed with furniture, Almus "Slim" Cox told how he rose from the bitterest poverty in Arkansas to sing down-home gospel songs heard around the world. Political insider and local comedian Mickey McTague related tales of Tom Eagleton, Bob Hope, and the events behind *The Exorcist.*

When the book went to press in the summer of 2010, I had no idea how big the response would be. The critics loved it, and not just because of the short, easy-to-read chapters. "If a transplant wants to understand the South Side, he or she should read Merkel's book," wrote Bill McClellan of the *Post-Dispatch.* I sold Mickey McTague six copies at a time. He'd give them to friends and come back for six more. My wife's hair stylist sold I don't know how many copies to her customers. I kept running into people who said they read it and loved it.

I moved on to write two other books for Reedy Press: *Beer, Brats, and Baseball: St. Louis Germans* and *The Making of an Icon: The Dreamers, the Schemers, and the Hard Hats Who Built the Gateway Arch.* Each has a special meaning for me. As I did with *Hoosiers,* with each book I made friends and learned things people didn't know before. As a fifth-generation German-American, I had a special joy writing *Beer, Brats, and Baseball.* Having grown up during the construction of the Gateway Arch, I loved putting together a book about the monument.

But *Hoosiers* has a place in my heart that no other book has. So when Reedy Press ran out of copies for me to sell to my wife's hair stylist, it could have printed some more. But it was time for an update. So I sought out more stories. Sadly, Slim Cox and Mickey McTague were gone, but others were there to tell their own stories. Former *Donnybrook* provocateur Martin Duggan told me about growing up on Connecticut Street, while former fire chief Neil Svetanics filled me in about the day Carondelet almost blew up. We dropped a few tales from the first edition, but I trust the new ones make the book that much richer. We've added quotes from old timers about the way things used to be on the South Side and a few updates. Here's hoping customers of my wife's hair stylist like the book, along with anybody else who likes to learn about the South Side. This South Side hoosier has gone to almost every length to make this book more informative and more fun. There are limits, though. I have no plans to ask people what a hoosier is. I still have memories of the brawny guy who asked me, "You callin' me a @*$%@*#$%@ hoosier?"

INTRODUCTION

With a mix of Cardinals and Anheuser-Busch memorabilia draping the walls, Ferguson's Pub at 2925 Mount Pleasant Street is as South Side as it gets. Throw in the fact that it is one of the last places to buy a genuine brain sandwich, and the restaurant should be a great inspiration when it comes to defining the South Side of St. Louis, as well as South Siders. A patron sat at the bar and tried to explain: "If you don't know what makes it the South Side, you're not a South Sider," he said. "If you weren't born and raised on the South Side, I can't explain it to you." The man's explanation may seem to be influenced by drink, but what he said makes sense. It's hard to explain what makes the South Side the South Side.

To be sure, South St. Louis City occupies a special place in the metropolitan St. Louis area. Whether they have relocated to Arnold, St. Charles, or Collinsville, people reared on the South Side always bring with them fond remembrances of life south of Highway 40. Most remember living in an old house in a lot so small they could look out a side window into their neighbor's window. They remember Ted Drewes, Carondelet Park, and Southtown Famous. If they're older, Cherokee Street and Casa Loma may come to mind. The city's mayor, himself a child of the South Side, has his own memories. "We had all kinds of personalities, people from different religious backgrounds," Francis G. Slay said in his office at city hall. He hesitated to characterize the South Sider: "Virtually any type of character you had on the South Side." Slay recalls the neighborhoods as tight, where everyone knew everybody. "It was, I think, a very good place to grow up and raise a family."

More than that, it was a place to feast on different neighborhoods close to each other. Carondelet is nothing like Shaw. The ranch homes of St. Louis Hills Estates are nothing like the two-story brick homes of Dutchtown. The mansions in Compton Heights look nothing like the frame houses in Bevo Mill. The international shopping district on South Grand Boulevard is much different from busy Hampton Avenue. It's said that if you don't like the weather in St. Louis, wait five minutes and it'll change. If you're driving on the South Side, you don't need five minutes. Wait a minute, and you'll see something new. There are few places in the metropolitan area with so many different kinds of neighborhoods set so close together.

History not only played a role in making these places so different, but it also brought factors that many held in common. One of the biggest was the Catholic faith. Another was race: the South Side is still heavily white. "You're talking about a white working class community," said Mark Abbott, a professor of history with urban emphasis at Harris-Stowe State University. He is a resident of the Tower Grove South neighborhood and the author of the book *Tower Grove*, about neighborhoods around Tower Grove Park. Abbott sees similarities between the South Side and parts of some other cities. Places in East Coast cities like South Philadelphia, South Boston, and Queens are among them, he said. "South Boston is very Irish. South Philly is pretty Italian," he said. South Milwaukee is another similar community, he said. Such places give rise to characters in politics, in churches, across the street. And characters lead to stories, some of which are repeated here.

In recent years, many of the stories had to do with how much of the South Side has turned itself around. Ten, twenty, thirty, and forty years ago, much of the South Side was in severe distress. But as many of the stories in this volume testify, one by one the neighborhoods, parks, and commercial districts breathed new life. Tax breaks and the work of the mayor and aldermen helped, but what really made it happen were individuals who saw the potential of their area and worked to improve it. One of the first was Lafayette Square. It went from an area full of tenements and prostitutes to a revitalized stately Victorian neighborhood set around a park. Ruth Kamphoefner's story is recounted in these pages and is representative of the many individuals who bought broken-down Victorian homes for next to nothing and devoted much of their lives to rehabbing them. The rehabbers went from home to home, saving them from demolition.

Tower Grove Park came back under Director John Karel. Immigrants and refugees with a vision turned the South Grand commercial district into a vibrant international shopping and restaurant mecca. Bosnian refugees who came in the 1990s are doing the same in the area around the Bevo Mill. Hispanics settled in the former shopping area of Cherokee Street west of Jefferson Avenue and made it their own. Those who see history in one-hundred-year-old tables and chairs turned Cherokee Street east of Jefferson into the best place in the region to look for antiques.

Young professionals did their part by purchasing, maintaining, and improving homes on the South Side, many of which were saved by rehabbers, who do their work on just about every street south of Highway 40. The work slowed considerably when the recession started. Condos went unsold, and previously announced projects never got started. But even in the worst of the recession, individuals assured that the South Side would keep improving. Everywhere the story is the same. The South Side still has a way to go, but those with negative impressions made decades ago may be surprised at what they discover when they drive around South St. Louis with open eyes for an afternoon.

It seems the days of emptying out have largely passed on the South Side. The suburbs are fine, if you like that, but those who remain prefer the urban life to the suburban. They like their homes close together and stop signs that really don't stop anybody. They like being minutes from Ted Drewes or the Hill. To them, life on the South Side is like going around all the time in their favorite pair of old shoes. As the guy in the bar said, that still may not explain what it means to be a South Sider. Maybe he's right. Maybe if you don't know what makes it the South Side, you're not a South Sider. Maybe if you weren't born and raised on the South Side, then nobody can explain it. For those who don't understand, the stories in this book may help. Those who do will find that the stories affirm their convictions. Read on.

*Bob Burnes addresses an audience
at a CSMAC groundbreaking.*

On a warm Saturday in April 2010, about two dozen people on the South Side of St. Louis paused to ponder a question many have considered before them. Just what exactly is a hoosier? "It's one of those things. It's like pornography. You know it when you see it," St. Louis Hills resident Courtney Wheaton said at a family picnic in Willmore Park. Holly Hills resident Mike Carril put down his vanilla shake at Ted Drewes to form an answer. They're "somebody that doesn't secure their property. They've just got bad habits. They're loud and rowdy." To Julie McNeal, a news editor for KSDK–Channel 5, "a hoosier is white trash. A hoosier would have his hair with short sides and top and long hair on the back and wear tight, tight jeans and high-topped tennis shoes," she said outside the Soulard Farmers Market. "They'd be very right-wing. Beer, guns, and ammo," the forty-year-old Benton Park resident said.

Nearby, Norma King, of the Compton Hill Reservoir Square neighborhood, offered that the term was derogatory. "I really don't like to pigeonhole people," she said. At the Time Out Bar and Grill, 3805 Meramec Street, a man named Glenn stopped watching a game between the Cardinals and the Mets to say the word means "trash." But then the Dutchtown-area man added that the word was unfair. "To be called a hoosier is an insulting term." Back in Willmore Park, a man took umbrage at the question. "You callin' me a (expletive) hoosier?"

The meaning is enough to start a fight in some places around here, but nowhere else. When people outside the St. Louis region think of the word, they conjure up the positive image of the Indiana hoosier, but that wasn't always so. Jeffrey Graf took time off from his job with the reference department of the Herman B. Wells Library of Indiana University–Bloomington to study how the word came to be, with all of its good and bad overtones. "The best evidence, however, suggests that 'hoosier' was a term of contempt and opprobrium common in the upland South and used to denote a rustic, a bumpkin, a countryman, a roughneck, a hick or an awkward, uncouth or unskilled fellow," he wrote. In other words, a South Side hoosier.

Graf offered various reasons for the way the word began. One is that when the state of Indiana was being laid out, surveyors who found the residence of a squatter would ask, "Who's here?" Others believe it is a derogatory word used in the South for an uncouth rustic. One possibility is that *hoosier* often was used throughout the South in the nineteenth century to mean woodsmen or rough hill people. A similar word, *hoozer,* is used in the dialect of Cumberland, England, for hill dwellers or highlanders. They settled in the Cumberland Mountains, Cumberland River, and Cumberland Gap and in the hills of southern Indiana.

As for the St. Louis exception to the generally good view of hoosiers, Graf points to a study by Kansas State University English professor Thomas E. Murray. "Few epithets in St. Louis carry the pejorative connotations or the potential for eliciting negative responses that hoosier does," Murray wrote. Some in St. Louis and on the South Side may see a hoosier as someone who has shown a bad side. Others may say that's unfair. A third group of South Siders holds on to the title "South Side hoosier." They don't mean it in the Indiana sense. They keep up their property as well as anyone but laugh at the idea of being associated with the uncouth. Mickey McTague, a lifetime South Sider who worked with politicians, entertainers, and others, saw the title as a way to connect with victims of bigotry. "South St. Louis has been unfairly defamed in many ways," he said. "I'm very proud to say that I'm a South Side hoosier."

Unquestionably, the word is derogatory, but in a time when most people have stopped using almost all derogatory names for racial, religious, or ethnic groups, this one remains in use on the South Side and in the rest of the area. It may be that the term doesn't refer to who people are but what the Reverend Martin Luther King Jr. called "the content of their character." Whatever it is, the description by blues musician Van Johnson of a hoosier is typical. "A hoosier is when they throw their trash out the window," the Carondelet neighborhood resident said, taking a break from playing for tips near the Soulard Farmers Market. "They don't cut their lawn. Basically, just people that like to barbecue every day, get fat, and do nothing."

A hapless Fuller Brush salesman once asked Florence Deppe if she wanted to buy a mop. Absolutely not, she replied. She gets down on her knees with a brush and does her cleaning that way, she told him. "He said, 'I hear the same story all along here,'" Deppe relayed. "Nobody in South St. Louis uses a mop," he said with a sigh. Deppe was just months from being 100 years old when she told the story about the ways of the South Side Scrubby Dutch. She related it one day in 2010 in the dining room of the St. Louis Altenheim, an assisted-living facility at 5408 South Broadway. It was lunchtime, and Deppe and other Altenheim residents were eating salad, melons, spaghetti, and cake near a floor-to-ceiling window with one of the best views of the Mississippi south of the Arch. All remembered living in South St. Louis in the early to middle part of the twentieth century, when people regularly cleaned steps and sometimes sidewalks with soapy brushes.

"Every Saturday, they'd get out there and scrub the sidewalks," said Betty Reinbold. Those who lived in flats with more than one tenant took turns. "If you didn't do it, you weren't worth anything," said Reinbold, who lived in a house on Minnesota Avenue that was later demolished by the builders of Interstate 55. She doesn't remember sidewalks being scrubbed as much as she remembers steps being scrubbed. "I don't think it mattered what they were. They got scrubbed." When she first married, she and her husband lived in a flat on Chippewa Street. They took turns cleaning the concrete steps. But she eased up when she and her husband bought a home on Austria Street. "I didn't scrub them. I washed them off with a hose."

Deppe recalled a man would come by every Saturday to scrub her family's concrete front porch with Bon Ami. "I think my mother gave him a dollar," she said. "Of course everybody on the block hired him and so the whole block had a fresh appearance." Virginia Palazzolo, who grew up on Hartford Street one block east of Grand, has memories of cleaning her family's porch, which was wooden on the top and concrete on the bottom. "We'd get on our hands and knees and scrub it with a brush," said Palazzolo. She believes the preferred soap was Fels Naptha. She also remembers that she used a hose and a broom for the concrete steps. "It was just in their heritage, I guess, to keep everything neat and clean."

Esley Hamilton, a historian working for St. Louis County, believes the Scrubby Dutch practice may hearken back to a time when people dragged a lot more dirt into the house. Hamilton, who specializes in the preservation of historic buildings, said the front limestone steps would have shown dirt more. "The streets were dirty. There were no paved streets," Hamilton said. Since there were no vacuum cleaners to suck up dirt, housewives wanted to scrub as much of it off the steps as they could before it had a chance to come in.

That may or may not have led people living around Marion Bolt's house to get on their knees and scrub slab concrete steps. After she married in 1937, she and her husband moved to a house at 4727 Parker Avenue. "They did it as far back as I can remember," Bolt said. "Every Friday they would be out scrubbing the steps." And what did they scrub the steps with? Dutch Cleanser, of course.

As a housewife in the late 1930s and early 1940s, Mary Tomazi got her exercise scrubbing sidewalks at her South Side home. Today, at 101, the North Hampton neighborhood resident exercises in yearly one-mile mature walks in Forest Park and at the St. Louis Activity Center at 5602 Arsenal Street. She's seen a century of changes on the South Side since she was born in 1913 and remembers all the landmarks way back when. "It's changed a lot. It's a younger group moving in," said Tomazi, seated at a table at the activity center. "The homes are pretty well taken care of, and I'm close to everything. I'm close to grocery stores, church, everything, I'm close to it."

Now a mother, grandmother, great grandmother and great-great grandmother, Tomazi began life as Mary Seper in a home at 4019 Clayton Ave., less than a half-block north of present-day Interstate 64. If that thoroughfare, which everyone in St. Louis calls "Highway 40," is the dividing line of South St. Louis and the rest of the city, she didn't grow up a South Sider. But she was close enough to take in what the South Side had to offer. She has memories of the Casa Loma dance hall on Cherokee Street and the Forest Park Highlands. "I went there. I was always dancing, going dancing. We always went in groups, going to dances." Of the Forest Park Highlands, she said, "I went there a lot. We always went in a group, girls and boys." She loved the dancing and swimming and hated to see it burn down in 1963.

She married John Tomazi in 1935 and moved into a home at 4056 Blaine Avenue, just west of Grand Boulevard and just north of present-day Interstate 44. There, she discovered a housewife had to fulfill certain obligations if the neighborhood was going to accept her. "We scrubbed our steps and sat outside and had coffee or beer," she said. "In the evening, we'd sit outside." She often went to the busy Cherokee Street shopping district. "There were all kinds of stores and confectioneries,

grocery stores." One store
she remembers well was Kohlberg's
Drugstore.

In the mid-1940s, her family moved to Richmond Heights
and stayed there until 1963. That's when they moved back
to the South Side, not far from the corner of Chippewa Street
and Hampton Avenue. It was a growing place, not far from
Hampton Village at Chippewa and Hampton and the Southtown Famous-Barr at Chippewa and Kingshighway. "That's
where I bought all my clothes then. I was always little. I had
a hard time to get clothes," she said. She remembers well the
pedestrian tunnel underneath Chippewa that connected the
department store to a parking lot about where the present-
day Shop 'n Save lot is now located.

Tomazi depended on her husband to get around until she
was seventy-nine, when he developed macular degeneration
in his eyes. "I thought, it's either learn how to drive, or we're
going to sit at home," she said. Not liking that second option, she
went to a driving school. "I told them then that I was an old lady,

never drove a car before in my life. I said they had a lot of nerve to teach me." She kept driving, even after her husband died on October 26, 2011, at the age of 102. With trepidation, at the age of 100, she came to a state license office to renew her license. The clerk was stunned when she learned Tomazi's age.

At her age, Tomazi doesn't drive much. She only goes to the Schnucks at Hampton Village Plaza, just a short distance from her home. To get to the St. Louis Activity Center, she takes a van. There's too many accidents, she said. "People are trying to beat the lights. I just come over here. They pick me up. They take me home, and I have a lot of fun on the bus seeing all the South Side."

Tomazi's attendance at the center is part of her secret for being so healthy at 101. "Be active. That's why instead of me being alone, I go to the senior center to be with people, not sit at home. I'm not a television watcher," she said. "I come here for the one-hour exercise." She's been coming since her husband died. She rarely visits the doctor and has her cholesterol well under control. She showed off what she could do at the Go! St. Louis Mature Mile walks in April 2013 and April 2014 in Forest Park. In April 2013, a piece on FOX 2 profiled her happily striding in the walk. She was holding a cane but not using it. That's for old folks.

Young Martin Duggan had it made. He pocketed a quarter to mop wooden porches around his South Side home, fifty cents to scrub stone steps with Dutch Cleanser or Bon Ami. A dime gained him entrance into the Ritz, a local movie emporium on South Grand Boulevard between Hartford and Juniata Streets. It's one of buckets full of happy memories Duggan has of the formative years he spent on the South Side. St. Louisans remember him best as the editorial page editor of the *Globe-Democrat* until 1984 and as the founding provocateur of *Donnybrook* on KETC–Channel 9 from 1987 to 2009. He remembers an earlier time when everybody walked or took the streetcar.

One of his favorite memories is of preparing ice cream concoctions in a neighborhood ice cream parlor three doors from his house. It helped him snatch the girl of his dreams. After more than seven decades of wedded bliss, Mae and Martin Duggan get around in wheelchairs, but otherwise are well and laughing at each other's jokes at the St. Agnes Home assisted living facility in Kirkwood.

Martin Duggan began life on June 3, 1921, as an Irishman in a German neighborhood. "In true South Side style, I was born in a four-family flat on Michigan Avenue," he said. "I was born on the first floor east, and it's still there."

9

When he was four, his family moved to 4108 Connecticut Street, in Holy Family Parish. When he tagged along with his mom and six-year-old sister to enroll in Holy Family School, a nun named Sister Hilaria looked at him and said, "Here's a fine big boy for kindergarten." Young Martin flinched at losing his freedom, but started that afternoon.

"In kindergarten, they had a lay woman, and no matter her real name, her name was Miss Marie," Martin said. During a May 2014 interview in Martin and Mae's apartment at St. Agnes Home, Martin demonstrated that his memory was still sharp at ninety-two by rattling off the names of each of his teachers at Holy Family. In order, they were: Sisters Hilaria, Mary Frances, Henrietta, Clementine, Mary Louis, Zita, Mary Frances (a second time), and Elizabeth. His father, whose parents were Irish immigrants, said this when grades came out: "I'd start to hand him my report card, and he'd say 'Which krauthead beat you this time?" Actually, he recalls, he was a decent fifth in his class.

"We lived in a neighborhood where everything was self-contained," Martin said. "In many cases, there were competing grocery stores on the same intersection." Grand Boulevard south of Arsenal Street was bustling, full of businesses like restaurants, bakeries, and the Tower Grove Bank. In spite of the Germans' domination of the neighborhood, the Irish were in charge of the political offices. They included State Representative Maurice Cleary, Alderman Phelim O'Toole and State Senator Jim Doran. "I didn't know there were any Republicans until I grew up," Duggan said.

Into this way of life arrived two interruptions—pleasant ones, mind you. The first came when Duggan's eighth grade teacher allowed him to tinker with the idea of starting a class newspaper. Nothing came of it. Then his sister started talking about a classmate she had at St. Joseph's Academy on the present grounds of Fontbonne University in Clayton. She lived on the North Side, and her name was Mae Mosher. The talk intrigued him. The girl paid a visit while Duggan was working at a neighborhood ice cream store between his freshman and sophomore years at South Side Catholic High School (now St. Mary's High School). "He delivered ice cream to me constantly," said that girl, who is now Mae Duggan. "I was smitten with her," Martin said.

At South Side Catholic, Martin moved up to editor of the school newspaper. He attended St. Mary's University in San Antonio, Texas, on a scholarship and eventually edited the school paper. In the summer, he worked for the *Globe-Democrat*. After three summers at the *Globe*, he received an offer during Christmas break of 1941 to work full-time. He grabbed at the opportunity and arranged to finish up at St. Louis University.

The two lovebirds married on May 26, 1942. Later that year, he joined the marines and spent much of the rest of the war editing stories written by combat correspondents for hometown papers. After the war, the Duggans moved to North St. Louis and later to Creve Coeur. While Martin moved up the ladder at the *Globe-Democrat,* Mae was a busy mother of five and an active leader of the school choice movement. They've done a lot, and Martin said his South Side upbringing helped. It put in him, he said, the importance of "being dependable in the sense of if you say you're going to do something, you do it."

Martin Duggan in front of 4108 Connecticut Street.

Back in 2000, people thought Guy Slay was crazy when he bought a ramshackle old department store building at a lonely corner of Manchester Avenue. "It was a mess. Every square inch from the basement up was filled with stuff, every square inch from the basement up to the second floor. It had been pretty much not open to the public for maybe two decades," he said. Most of the surrounding buildings were abandoned and boarded up. "I personally didn't have anything stolen from my car. The contractors I was working with, they had stuff stolen from their cars."

Slay had to speak up when he uttered those words one summer day in 2014 in the building he had purchased and rehabbed on the southeast

corner of Tower Grove Avenue and Manchester. It was four on a Friday afternoon in the summer, and a happy crowd was chowing down on soul food provided by Slay's main tenant, Sweetie Pie's at the Mangrove. It's one of two Sweetie Pie's restaurants made famous by a reality show on the Oprah Winfrey Network, so the crowd likely included folks from throughout the country.

Slay was one of a number of rehabbers, business people, neighbors, and others who worked to turn around the mile-long strip of Manchester and Chouteau Avenues between Vande- venter Avenue and Kingshighway Boulevard. On both ends of the neighborhood, a sign hangs over the street, with the words "The Grove," the name the strip has received in recent years. At night, visitors come to an area with sixteen bars that close at 3 A.M., the highest concentration of such bars in the city. The Grove is home to places such as Atomic Cowboy, Attitudes Night Club, and Bad Dog Bar and Grill. Many of them are gay bars, continuing a trend that started in the 1990s. The entertainment district that emerged from the turnabout is a much different place from the one old timers remember,

Whatever the name, it was a bustling shopping district sixty years ago, with a Schnucks, a movie theater, clothing stores, and other shops. Carp's Department Store was in the building now occupied by Sweetie Pie's. The area around the Grove, called the Forest Park Southeast neighborhood, was one of the city's first suburbs. "It had a streetcar line that came to this area. It has always been a working class area," said Brooks Goedeker. He's the executive director of Park Central Development, a develop- ment and marketing agency for the area. Decline started in the 1960s and sped up in the decades that followed. Businesses used empty storefronts along Manchester for cheap warehouse and garage space.

Hopes for the area seemed grim. After working to improve the Central West End and an area between Kingshighway, Manchester, Taylor Avenue, and I-64, the Washington University Medical Center Redevelopment Corporation turned its atten- tion to the Forest Park Southeast neighborhood when a teen- ager died in a drive-by shooting in the mid-1990s. Since 1996, it has spent more than $30 million on the neighborhood. Today, there are a few boarded-up buildings, but there are many more brightly painted, with hand-painted scenes and eighteen murals. While only about eight of about one hundred buildings in the strip had businesses in them in 2002, about seventy-five now are filled, Goedeker said.

The work of pioneering rehabbers like Slay was key. As he saw it, the corner was busy, but there was no place to stop. So from March 2004 to March 2005, he operated the Mangrove Café and Ice Cream Parlor at the intersection to give people a reason to stop. (If you didn't know, "Mangrove" is short for "Manchester and Tower Grove.") Then, in July 2005, Sweetie Pie's agreed to move in.

The success of the investment in that corner and other places on the strip spread. "The last couple of years has really taken off," said Slay, who owns about fifteen properties in the Grove. Among his tenants in those properties are Sheryl and James Myers, owners of the City Boutique at the southwest corner of Manchester and Tower Grove. It's a colorful place full of multicolored dresses, tops, rompers, and shoes. "I like it because it's diverse. This is a very diverse neighborhood," Sheryl said. Among Slay's other tenants are a handbag boutique, a salon, and a nonprofit local foods market. He claims the success of the area is the result of the work of a wide variety of independent businesses and entrepreneurs who used their creativity and different perspectives to restore the area. Like many in the Grove, they gambled right that the future was bright in an area that everybody else had written off.

A SOUTH SIDER TO THE END

Nobody doubted Jim Fox's allegiance. When he moved back to St. Louis from Bloomington, Illinois, to take a newspaper job, his wife wanted to check out the North Side. His response: "'No way,' I said. She had never heard the expression you can take the South Side out of the boy, but you cannot take the boy out of the South Side," he wrote in the *South Side Journal*. "The Central West End and the North Side—you can have them. My heart belongs to South St. Louis," he wrote in a column for the *Suburban Journals*.

When Fox died at the age of ninety-one in January 2014, many who long had read his columns knew they had lost a friend. In his last column, printed four days after his death, he talked about the fire stations he knew about when he was growing up on the South Side. "My dad was a fire buff," he wrote in that final column. "When I was a kid he used to take me to the firehouse on Rutger and Jefferson maybe three times a week. Back in those days, the firemen had teams of three horses which would pull one truck."

Fox grew up on Hartford Street, south of Tower Grove Park, and ran around in street gangs. Not to worry, though, he wrote in one column: "We called them gangs, but they were really a collection of kids doing goofy things." Gangs would play games like red light, green light. "You would run to a certain line and if the guys on the other side yelled 'red light,' you had to stop, and if they yelled 'green light,' you could keep going."

Fox started in the news biz at sixteen, when he edited a newspaper at a Boy Scout camp. He graduated from Roosevelt High School and then received his English degree from Washington University. He started his first newspaper job at the Bloomington, Illinois, *Pantagraph* in 1943, returned to St. Louis in 1950 to take a position at the old *Star-Times*, and moved over to the *Post-Dispatch* the next year. He retired in 1984, but kept writing a column for that paper until 1993. He began writing a column for the *South County* and *South Side Journals* after that. When macular degeneration robbed him of much of his eyesight, he dictated his columns to his wife, "Friend Wife" Marty, a favorite subject in his columns. When she died after sixty-seven years of marriage in 2012, his daughter-in-law Cindy Fox took over the job.

For many who plucked their *Journal* from their front yard each week, Fox's column named "Fox Tales" was the first thing they read. Readers who knew him could imagine him smiling and laughing as he wrote. His columns for the *Suburban Journals* were rich in details about his childhood on the South Side. "For instance, every self-respecting drug store had a soda fountain. Whenever I could catch a dime from my dad, I would go to Petti's Pharmacy at Juniata and Oak Hill for a milk shake," he wrote. "I think he lost money on me. He had to put in ice cream, milk and flavoring and he threw in a couple of cookies." He wrote with nostalgia about the passing of the revolving Vess soda bottle at Gravois and Hampton Avenues and such long-gone movie shows as the Shenandoah, the Melba, and the Ritz.

A call from a reader led him to write about the old miniature golf course and driving range at Juniata Street and Kingshighway. "I remember the golf course because in the 1930s, miniature golf courses sprung up all over the country," he wrote. "I think it cost about a quarter to play nine holes. I don't remember the driving range, but I remember a softball park at that intersection. It cost 10 cents to get in and you saw two games, first a women's game, then a men's game. I don't know why we paid to watch softball because we played it all day."

Although Jim and Marty Fox lived much of their adult lives in Affton, he often wrote about eating at the Buttery, a restaurant on South Grand Boulevard just north of Chippewa. Staffers at the *South Journals* looked forward to their occasional lunches with the Foxes at the Steak 'n Shake at Gravois and Hampton Avenues. Over Steakburgers and Chili 3-Way, they would hear some gentle wisdom dispensed with a chortle and perhaps a story or two about a time long gone on the South Side.

TV FOR THE REJECTS

Holding a mike in front of the St. Louis Psychiatric Rehabilitation Center, Pete Parisi looked like he might be preparing for a hard-hitting TV report on mental illness. Until he opened his mouth. "We're at 5400 Arsenal St., otherwise known as the nuthouse, where mentally retarded and mentally ill people of the state of Missouri are housed," he said, in front of the wrought iron fence around the hospital. In the background is the music of the widely-criticized 1960s song about mental illness, "They're Coming to Take Me Away, Ha-Haaa!" Parisi then talks about a great dinner held at the hospital the night before. "It was a great dinner. It was a beautiful feast, like seven or eight courses and everything in it from soup to nuts."

It was outrageous, of course, but typical of what you could expect in the fifteen years the South Side resident was a favorite of local public access cable station viewers in the 1980s, 1990s, and the start of the new millennium. Those watching his show, *World Wide Magazine*, got used to seeing him getting tossed from everything from the St. Louis victory party for Bill Clinton's re-election to the old VP Fair. But to that South Sider, it just made the show better. "When people cover over the camera, we love it, because it makes them look so bad," he said as he was told to leave. That happened a lot in the show, which was as much theater of the absurd as it was TV documentary. Many of the segments are still drawing viewers on YouTube.

Anything could happen in the unscripted segments of *World Wide Magazine*. "He was real direct and blunt about things. That's what made him interesting, I guess, because he would state the obvious," said Hill neighborhood resident Bruce Marren, a videographer who knew Parisi. "There was one (show) where he broke up with his girlfriend, and they were screaming and yelling at each other." With him would come such characters as Black Jesus and Vladimir Noskov as the Mad Russian. "It seemed he had that New York jerk kind of personality, but kind of likable," said Mike Algarda. Algarda worked at a TV repair shop where Parisi would bring in equipment for repair. He sometimes went to Parisi's apartment and watched him edit film. Morton Hill had mixed feelings about Parisi. Hill was the program director at Double Helix, which produced material for public access channels. As such, he saw Parisi as a pain because of the way he was always challenging FCC regulations. On the other hand, "He was a great guy."

A New Jersey native, Parisi started in 1969 at a Springfield, Massachusetts, radio station and became program manager of the old progressive radio station KADI in 1971. While Parisi was at KADI, the *Riverfront Times* noted in 2002, he played a cruel joke on his preschool niece and nephew that showed even then his lack of taste. On a visit home to New Jersey on Christmas Eve, he played them a cassette tape he'd produced. But they thought they were listening to a radio broadcast announcing that Santa Claus had died in a fiery plane crash. Niece and nephew broke down in tears.

Fired in 1983, he started work as a film editor at St. Louis's Channel 1. In 1986, he started showing stuff he'd shot on local public access channels. Audiences were kind as *World Wide Magazine* developed an audience, but he had one enemy. A diabetic, he never took care of himself. Doughnuts were a favorite food. His health started sliding, and it was harder for him to carry a camera. His production declined. In November 2001, while in Florida, he slipped into a diabetic coma. He died in January 2002, at the age of 54.

In a 1997 interview with the *Post-Dispatch*, Parisi summed up the meaning of *World Wide Magazine* this way: "The whole show, if you really watch it, the whole show is based on unhappiness, sadness, society's rejects." Among those rejects, he said, was himself. He never made any money on *World Wide Magazine*. But if he was producing the same kind of material today, Algarda claims, he would be making plenty by showing it on YouTube. "Parisi today would probably be a multimillionaire," Algarda said. But if Parisi did, the program might change, because he would no longer be among the rejects.

The sight had Johnny Carson and his audience roaring with laughter. Stan Kann nervously fidgeted as he tried to demonstrate his collection of ancient vacuum cleaners. But the more he tried, the more things went wrong. The more he pumped the nineteenth-century machines, the more they left grime on the floor. More than four decades later, a video of the same program set folks at the eightieth anniversary program of the Holly Hills Improvement Association to guffawing. So did the stories he told those who attended the program.

It was more than just an act for Kann, who grew up in St. Louis, moved to Hollywood in 1975, and moved back to spend the last decade of his life on Federer Place on the South Side. "He could play any music," longtime friend Judy Brilliante told a reporter for the *South Side Journal* after he died in 2008 at the age of eighty-three. "He knew it in his head. He had it. But if you asked him where he parked his car, forget it." Ed Schroeder, director of volunteer services at the Fabulous Fox, said that was the way it was when Kann played at the theater from 1999 to the night before he died. Kann needed a space to park his car, an organ to play his music, and an abundant supply of napkins to wipe up all the coffee he spilled.

That's pretty much how Kann kept coming back to Johnny Carson after that first fumble-filled appearance in 1965 turned into a regular gig. Altogether, he made seventy-seven guest appearances on Carson's show, eighty-nine on the old *Mike Douglas Show*, and thirty-two on the *Merv Griffin Show*. He also had a syndicated show in Canada for three years, was a character in two situation comedies, and played the organ as background for the television series M*A*S*H. But he spent his younger years on Washington Avenue, collecting vacuum cleaners and honing his musical talents. As he built his reputation locally, he played the organ at the old Fox Theatre and at Ruggeri's Restaurant from 1953 to 1975. The local older set will remember him as co-host of TV's *The Noon Show* with Marty Bronson and as a regular on the *Charlotte Peters Show*.

It was through those appearances that he made friends with slapstick comedienne Phyllis Diller, who lived in Webster Groves at the time. Bemused by Kann's collection of more than a hundred old vacuums, she persuaded Carson to have him on his show. That's where the miscues began. As Kann told it, he was waiting to go on when somebody told him to go downstairs to makeup. He went through a door marked "exit" and closed the door behind him. That put him on a fire escape with no way back in. So he made his way down seven floors and into a tunnel that ended across the street from the building that he had been in. He desperately worked through the crowd and got upstairs again. The makeup that was hurriedly applied to his face couldn't hide his sense of panic. He intended to give a serious demonstration. "But instead of appearing like a museum docent showing an exhibit, he came off like a flustered character out of Dr. Seuss," the *South Side Journal* said in a profile. But that wasn't necessarily bad. "It opened up a whole new career," he told the paper in an interview at his home, not far from his collection of old sucking machines.

Kann had a perfect comedic sense, especially when comics like Carson and Bill Cosby played straight men. He loved to joke with his neighbors on Federer Place. "He just had a tremendous sense of humor," neighbor Bernice Mueller said after he died. At night when she and her husband, Norman, sat on their porch, Kann would join them. "He could come out with some doozy sayings sometimes, kind of twist his words around. He was really funny." The vacuum cleaners looked strange, Bernice Mueller said. But, she said, "He helped us by being such a good neighbor and friend. He had a heart as big as himself."

Father Robert Arnold decided things had gone too far. It was the late 1940s, and students at St. John the Baptist High School were hanging out after school at a nearby café on Gravois Avenue, not far from the Bevo Mill. "He didn't think we should be meeting in a place like that," said Beverly Spinner, a member of the school's class of 1950. So Arnold, the associate pastor of St. John the Baptist Church came by one day and threw them out. "We were back the next day," Spinner said. "We were just talking and having sodas."

Spinner is one of a group of female members of that class who have met regularly for lunch since they graduated from the high school at 5021 Adkins Avenue. At one time, as many as twenty-five female members of the co-ed class met regularly at a local restaurant. The men stayed away. But only eight of them came to a gathering at Bill Gianino's in Oakville in May 2014. So most brought their husbands.

Those at the luncheon could remember attending a high school that had 440 students. In the year the high school reached that level—1949—the grade school had 880 students. Already, St. John the Baptist School had made much history. On September 1, 1914, 235 grade school students came to the first opening day of school for what was then known as Oak Hill Catholic Parish. It was just six months after the Rev. John Peters celebrated the first Mass in a storefront at 4626 Gravois Avenue. Parishioners moved fast to build a permanent home for their new church. On Thanksgiving Day 1914, Archbishop John Glennon celebrated the first Mass for the new church at 4200 Delor Street. Fifteen years later, in September 1929, the school started classes for high school students.

Rev. Peters still was pastor when members of the class of 1950 attended St. John the Baptist High School. Over olive salad and tilapia, alums at the May 2014 gathering at Bill Gianino's spoke about the priest's generosity. He bought shoes for students who didn't have any good ones and allowed them to attend school for free if their parents didn't have jobs. A story told by class of 1950 alum

Here and There

A page from the 1950 St. John the Baptist High School yearbook

Lois Kennedy indicates Peters once was overly generous. He forgave the tuition of a student who said his father wasn't working. Later, though, it turned out that the father wasn't working because he was on vacation.

Students had mixed opinions about the nuns who taught almost all of their classes. A nun once sent Pat Vogel home because she thought her outfit was too revealing. The mother had reason to disagree, since she made it. "They'd throw an eraser at you or hit you on the head with a book to get your attention," Spinner said. But that doesn't mean Spinner thinks they were mean. "They were strict, but—I don't know—they treated you well," she said.

Whatever they thought of the discipline, the former St. John the Baptist High School students said they enjoyed attending the school. "I liked it because I knew everybody," Spinner said. She lived a few blocks away and started in kindergarten. She has pleasant memories of a nun who taught her in second and eighth grades. In high school, she loved history, spelling, and English but hated math. Out of class, she played softball and volleyball.

One of Mary Schaeffer's main memories was of bus rides from her home in Affton when she went to the school in her senior year. Delores Fleischmann took the Delor bus when she attended the school from her sophomore to senior years. She attended Rosati-Kain High School her freshman year, and liked that better. "It was all girls, and you wore uniforms," Fleischmann said. It was a "whole different atmosphere." Katherine Dunivin offers a long list of things she liked at St. John. "I thoroughly had a good time, and I met a lot of my friends here," said Dunivin, who lived just two blocks away.

These days, Catholic kids in the St. John the Baptist Parish and elsewhere won't experience what Dunivin and other students at the school went through. The high school closed in 2008 and the elementary school in 2014. They were part of a long list of Catholic schools that shut their doors on the South Side and elsewhere as parents sent their kids elsewhere. It's not easy for people like Dunivin to take. "That was a sad day for me," she said.

THE HORSE THIEVES OF CARONDELET

The town of Carondelet developed just to the south of St. Louis, but at a much slower pace. Some Carondelet families take pride in the fact that they can trace their lineage back to the independent nineteenth-century township. For the most part, the history of the town and these families is rich and vibrant, but there was a devious side. The evidence comes from "Carondelet Yesterday and Today," an unpublished manuscript written in 1933 that is on the shelves of the St. Louis Public Library's Central Branch. The author, A. Ryrie Koch, wrote that robbery and horse thievery were problems in Carondelet as early as 1840. One Frenchman named Louis was especially frightening to horse owners. "If a man was riding one that this desperado fancied, it was worth the rider's life if he did not give it up," Koch wrote. He was gone by 1846, when the citizenry could rest.

Koch also told of a company of horse thieves, led by a man named Sanspeur, who brought the citizenry endless grief. Whenever someone's horse was missing, Sanspeur would appear and offer to find it, for a small fee of five dollars. The man who paid the money would be led to another person who would offer to help find it for another fee of five dollars. "After this had been repeated several times, the horse would be returned but usually in such a poor condition that the animal would not be worth the many five dollars paid," Koch wrote. When they were done stealing horses, the rogues had children who had children whose descendants today have yet to discover their ancestors' occupations.

A FAILED VISION

In the 1840s, Charles Dickens added to his fame by writing about the cruelty of industrialization. Reformers reacted to that cruelty in different ways. Kark Marx thought communism would cure the excesses. Others formed communities they thought would be free of the evil they witnessed. Etienne Cabet—a politician, lawyer, and writer—published a utopian novel around 1839 titled *Voyage en Icarie*. His vision for a perfect life brought him thousands of followers. Some traveled to America to follow their dreams in Icarian communities. One group settled south of the present intersection of Hampton Avenue and Interstate 44.

In 1848, another group of Cabet's followers arrived in the Red River valley of Texas. That land was too unhealthy to live in, but soon Cabet came to join them. They traveled to the former Mormon settlement of Nauvoo, Illinois, to establish their community. A branch settlement was established in Adams County, Iowa. However, many members saw Cabet's leadership style as dictatorial. In 1856, a majority of the Nauvoo community expelled Cabet. He brought about 180 of his followers to St. Louis, but died shortly after they arrived.

Members stayed to build the kind of community Cabet envisioned. They worked in St. Louis to provide for the community. In the spring of 1858, they bought property called Cheltenham, six miles west of St. Louis, around the present location of Wilson Avenue east of Sulphur Avenue. They put $8,000 down on the $25,000 cost of the land and made regular monthly payments. They published a newspaper distributed around the world. But Icaria wouldn't last. Members started squabbling and leaving. The community fell behind on its mortgage. The end of the vision came in March 1864 when the mortgage holder demanded the group either pay or give the land back. The Icarians couldn't pay and left the land. So ended the dream of the St. Louis Icarians.

SECRET WEAPONS IN CARONDELET

People here know James B. Eads as the man who did something the experts said couldn't be done: build a bridge across the Mississippi at St. Louis. Down south, he is known for ridding the Mississippi south of New Orleans of sandbars that clogged the river. That enabled New Orleans to become a major port. A third accomplishment is often overlooked. On the river in Carondelet, he made weapons that were key to the Union's control over the Mississippi River during the Civil War. Ironclads made at shipyards in Carondelet that fought their way past Confederate positions on the Mississippi, Ohio, and lesser rivers were impervious to the iron balls that cannons heaved at them.

Before the war, this self-taught engineer made his fortune salvaging sunken steamboats from the bottom of the river. He had retired and was looking forward to a life of leisure. But soon after Confederates fired on Fort Sumter in April 1861, Eads started arguing that a fleet of armored gunboats could help open the Mississippi River. Five days later, he received a telegram from a friend from St. Louis, U.S. Attorney General Edward Bates: "Be not surprised if you are called here suddenly by telegram." Eads's ideas won over Lincoln's cabinet. On August 7, 1861, Eads signed a contract to build seven gunboats ready for crews and arms within sixty-five days.

To build his boats, Eads leased some existing yards from Marceau Street to Catalan Street in the city of Carondelet. Called the Carondelet Marine Railway, it was established in 1857 as a place for building and repairing riverboats. He established another yard at Mound City, Illinois, on the Ohio River near Cairo. At those yards, he set about to build seven ironclad gunboats named for communities on the upper Mississippi and Ohio Rivers. Boats made at Carondelet were key to the Union victory at the Confederate Fort Henry on the Tennessee River on February 6, 1862. It was more than a month before the Confederate ironclad *Merrimack* and the Union ironclad *Monitor* fought to a famous draw on March 8–9, 1862, at Hampton Roads, Virginia. Eads's boats went on to help win victories at Fort Donelson on the Cumberland River and elsewhere.

Anywhere from several hundred to four thousand people toiled at the Carondelet works. Ron Bolte, who heads the Carondelet Historical Society, speculates the number was closer to two thousand. The works kept turning out iron boats that pushed south as Admiral David G. Farragut made his way northward from New Orleans. When a siege was broken at Vicksburg in July 1863, all of the river was in Union hands, but boats still were needed to go up smaller waterways in Arkansas. In 1863, Eads bought land on the river in Carondelet from Davis Avenue to Poepping Street. Carondelet promised Eads wouldn't have to pay property taxes if he stayed for five years. Bolte compares it to today's tax increment financing, in which tax money meant for schools or police instead is used for bonds for a shopping center or other project receiving special government incentives.

Eventually, Eads produced about two dozen boats that helped shorten the war. After he stopped producing boats when the war ended in 1865, Carondelet sued Eads for failing to live up to his part of the deal on the tax break. The city lost. In 1870, St. Louis swallowed the community. Meanwhile, the ironclads were used for scrap. One survived—the *Cairo*—but only because it sank after it hit a Confederate mine on December 12, 1862, north of Vicksburg. By being on the bottom of the river, it avoided those hungry for scrap. After the *Cairo* was found in 1956 under river silt, it was brought to the surface and placed on display at the Vicksburg Military Park in 1977. But it is not necessary to travel to Vicksburg to learn the significance of what the ironclads did on the Mississippi. The Carondelet Historical Society has a thorough exhibit on Eads's boats at its headquarters at 6303 Michigan Avenue. A plaque at South St. Louis Square Park at South Broadway and Courtois Street also speaks of his accomplishment in opening the Mississippi during the Civil War. South Siders can say with pride that Carondelet was the place where he performed this act to shorten the war.

LAUNCHED OCT. 12TH 1861.
ARMAMENT 13 GUNS

Eng'd by

ST LOUIS o

THE FI

C° N York.

N DE KALB,

CONSTRUCTED BY
JAMES B. EADS.

ONCLAD.

29

A CONFEDERATE ATTACK OR A FLIGHT OF FANCY

It wasn't exactly the Battle of Gettysburg, and it wasn't even a Civil War skirmish, but if the raid at the home of Cheltenham postmaster Augustus Muegge really happened, it would have meant Confederate guerillas penetrated the future borders of St. Louis just months before the Civil War was over. A newspaper that repeated the official report of the incident also suggested that other factors may have clouded Muegge's memory. Muegge claimed the raid happened between 5 and 6 P.M. on Wednesday, September 28, 1864, at his home, general store, and post office on Manchester Road. Had it not been torn down in 1905, that home today would be at 6429 Manchester Avenue, on the corner of Dale Avenue. The Muegges had built their store and home in 1854 in an area surrounded by slave-holding Southern planters. As the postmaster, Muegge was seen as a Lincoln man.

This may have made him think the worst was coming when, he said, four men wearing regular Confederate uniforms rode to his door. As the *Missouri Republican* reported in its October 1, 1864, edition, two of those men got off their horses and went into the store while two others stayed outside with the horses. The two asked Muegge which side he was on. "I am a Union man," the *Missouri Republican* reported Muegge as saying. Then they asked him if he had held office in Lincoln's government. "Yes—I hold office now. I am Postmaster here," Muegge answered. "It's just such men as you that we want to kill," one of the two supposedly said.

Then one of them pulled out a revolver, cocked it, and pointed it at Muegge. Before he could shoot, Muegge's wife got between them and said that he'd have to kill her first. When the man tried to point over her shoulder, she pushed the firearm away. Muegge ran out the door, found a horse, and rode it to a military camp on Olive Street Road. There he told his tale and said a similar group had been at a home two miles away. Apparently, some didn't believe him. "Owing to the great delay on account of the incredibility of the story, the statement was not reported at headquarters until Friday morning," the *Missouri Republican* said. Then a scout was sent out. The *Missouri Republican* speculated that the Confederates were part of a group harassing the Pacific Railroad running west along Manchester, but it also noted that it was hard for Confederates to cross the fords and bridges along the Meramec River, since they all were well guarded. "The most plausible explanation is that the fright of the Postmaster induced him to imagine a great deal more than he saw and in his statement drew largely on his fancy," the paper said. If nothing else, it made for a good story of how a postmaster far from the fighting got involved in the battle to preserve the Union.

A LAWSUIT FOR HENRY SHAW

Henry Shaw never married, but the man who founded the Missouri Botanical Garden did have woman problems. One woman in particular sued him for a fortune for what she claimed was fudging on a promise to marry her. If she had won, the garden might not have looked as grand in its early years. The story shows the dangers of renting a piano to just any lady.

The tale is told in *Henry Shaw: His Life and Legacies* by renowned Saint Louis University historian Father William Barnaby Faherty, S.J. In 1856, Shaw, a wealthy retired St. Louis hardware baron, prepared to open a botanical garden at his country home outside St. Louis. In February of that year, a woman named Effie Carstang borrowed one hundred dollars from Shaw. He had met her the year before and seemed fascinated by her loveliness. The next year, she borrowed an additional one hundred dollars from him. Then in August 1857, she rented a piano from Shaw for one dollar a month.

It seemed harmless enough. But on July 19, 1858, she filed a suit in the St. Louis Court of Common Pleas for breach of promise of marriage. She asked for twenty thousand dollars in damages but then raised her demand to one hundred thousand dollars. She claimed they had promised to marry in 1856 after a friendship grew into romance. Shaw denied he had made any such promise. Effie and her sister contended the piano was a gift. If it was, Shaw took it back.

The two sides met in court on May 27, 1859, less than a month before the Missouri Botanical Garden opened. Effie was represented by criminal lawyer and state legislator Major Uriel L. Wright. Shaw's legal team included Edward Bates, who later became attorney general under President Abraham Lincoln. The jury heard testimony that Shaw had given Effie gifts of the piano, a book on botany, valuable jewelry, and fruits from his garden. He named a marriage date and then turned her away, she said. Shaw's attorney's sought to besmirch her character by producing a witness who said she lived at a place where "dashing fellows" lived. The jury deliberated and ruled in Effie's favor. Effie was awarded the one hundred thousand dollars she requested.

Shaw appealed. The next trial, in March 1860, made national news. Shaw's lawyers put forth a case that Effie had sought out Shaw to entrap him. Depositions from men in Brooklyn, Cincinnati, and Charleston said she was a prostitute. Judge Sam Reber wouldn't allow testimony that disputed those contentions. The second verdict went to Shaw, and he kept his one hundred thousand dollars. The court turned down Effie's request for another trial on the basis that some of the jurors were prejudiced. As far as the court was concerned, she was the nineteenth-century equivalent of the woman who fakes a neck injury in a car crash to get money out of the other driver.

The outcome left one question unanswered: had Effie won, how would it have affected Shaw's plans for his botanical garden? He had amassed a fortune of $250,000 when he retired in 1839. Losing to Effie would have sucked nearly half that amount out of Shaw's pocket. Botanical Garden archivist Andy Colligan believes a verdict against Shaw may have postponed some of the development of the grounds and the buildings. He cautions that it's all speculation, but it's a worthy question because it concerns a woman who was either a gold digger or a bride jilted at the altar.

Like many youngsters, William Ittner hated going to school. But almost alone among that group, Ittner was able to change what he hated about getting an education in St. Louis schools after the Civil War. Born in 1864, he detested the dark buildings of the city schools, especially their hallways. They lacked indoor plumbing, there were too few exits, and basement classrooms were dirty. He thought they were prisons.

The son of a prominent businessman and congressman, Ittner grew up to be an architect whose work included high-end homes in Compton Heights and Fox Park. He might have kept designing fine homes if a new office hadn't opened up on the St. Louis Board of Education. He was elected the board's commissioner of school buildings in 1897.

It was a time of explosive growth, in an era when the leadership of the city schools was progressive. Ittner designed forty-nine schools for the city, but not just any schools. He opened up the buildings and allowed light to bathe the interiors, even the basements. His floor plans were such that corridors had windows on the sides and not just on the ends. That eliminated the darkened hallways. He took advantage of generous budgets to put up buildings that would still be gems a century later. Today, the South Side is filled with those architectural jewels, including Cleveland, Fanning, Gardenville, McKinley, Mullanphy, and Oak Hill.

Ittner resigned as commissioner in 1910 and remained as "consulting architect" to the board until 1914. He went on to design hundreds of school buildings throughout the country and see his ideas become a standard for school architecture. Before he died in 1936, he designed the Missouri Athletic Club in 1916, the Scottish Rite Cathedral in 1921, and the Continental Building in 1929.

Today, the firms of William B. Ittner, Inc., and Ittner & Bowersox, Inc., carry his namesake. Many school buildings throughout the city and the country carry his legacy. In recent years, the St. Louis Public Schools have targeted many of the local ones for closing. Those who have protested have done so not only because the buildings are old, but because they are beautiful and lift the spirit. It's a fitting tribute to someone who sought to bring light to the dark parts of a student's day.

THE MAN BEHIND ST. LOUIS HILLS

In much of the rest of the South Side, it's common to have a mix of houses, stores, building materials, and building styles. Frame homes often are next to brick corner stores. But in St. Louis Hills, consistency is the norm. Almost every home and apartment is solid brick. There are no stores or offices off the primary thoroughfares. Even the schools, churches, and parks match the rest of the neighborhood.

The man responsible for that consistent appearance is Cyrus Crane Willmore. After developing homes in Normandy, University City, and Webster Groves in the county and Kingshighway Hills in the city in the early 1920s, he decided seven hundred acres of dairy farmland in St. Louis's southwest corner were ready for development. The property already had a history. David R. Francis, who is best known as the president of the 1904 World's Fair, bought it in 1884. In 1916, he donated sixty acres of the land for Francis Park.

Willmore started laying out Francis's former property just before the start of the Great Depression. The Depression could have given him reason to allow contractors who bought his land to do shoddy work that would bring prices down, but he insisted on exceptionally high standards of workmanship and architecture through the economic squeeze that threatened to break him. To bring a variety of income levels, he provided space for apartments, duplexes, small homes, and high-end homes, as well as schools and churches. To add to the neighborhood, he donated seventy acres of his land for Willmore Park in 1946. The project continued for several years after Willmore died in 1949. St. Louis Hills Estates, which was finished in the 1950s, features ranch homes instead of the two-story houses in the original development.

Willmore's plan for an area with quality homes and "country living in the city" became a reality. St. Louis Hills has grown into a premier neighborhood in the St. Louis metropolitan area. For this, South Siders can thank a man who insisted on maintaining the highest standards at the risk of his own personal fortune.

Cyrus Willmore, second from left, poses with dignitaries outside his office in St. Louis Hills

For eight decades, one of the most popular and consistently funny comic strips has been a tale of family life, keeping ahead of the boss, and the pursuit of the world's biggest sandwich. The comic is *Blondie*, and its themes can be traced back more than ninety years to McKinley High School when creator Murat Bernard "Chic" Young attended the school.

Young showed that budding talent in cartoons he created from 1915 to 1919 for McKinley's *Carnation*, a publication that looked like a yearbook, except that it came out twice a year. His style wasn't much different from the *Blondie* cartoons that first appeared in 1930. One, titled "Vacations," shows campers, a man hurriedly eating in the best Dagwood fashion, and a student pulling weeds in the Missouri Botanical Garden. To the student picking weeds, a man shouts, "Hey, you're pickin' our valuable

prune plant." Another cartoon shows McKinley battling Soldan High School in debate and football. "McKinley nearly talks Soldan's ears off in a debate," one panel says. In another panel, a player kicks a field goal from the 40-yard line. "Oh, isn't he cute," somebody says from the stands. And for those who think Young could only draw, he was also librarian of the McKinley Literary Society. The experience he gained at McKinley made the efforts of Dagwood to take uninterrupted naps even funnier and were among the steps he took to make *Blondie* one of the most popular strips ever.

After Young's death in 1973, his son, Dean Young, and John Marshall took over the strip. Today, *Blondie* appears in more than two thousand newspapers around the world. Perhaps remembering the influence of those McKinley High School days, Dean Young drew a cartoon in 2004 for McKinley's centennial. As Dagwood holds a huge sandwich with candles on top, Blondie says, "Dagwood made this in honor of the McKinley High School Centennial Celebration in 2004."

If anyone had asked Dagwood "the St. Louis question" about where he went to high school, he might have answered, "I'm a McKinley Goldbug."

World War II pinup girl Betty Grable is remembered locally with a star on the St. Louis Walk of Fame at 6350 Delmar Avenue, but the star could just as easily have been at the spot near where she lived at 3858 Lafayette Avenue after she was born in 1916. That house and the surrounding houses on the south side of Lafayette were demolished to make way for Interstate 44. The star could have been in front of the nearby Mullanphy School at 4221 Shaw Boulevard, where she first attended school. Or it could have been at her first church, St. John's Episcopal, at 3664 Arsenal Street. The Reverend Killian Stimpson baptized her at the church on March 26, 1921. Church records say her sponsors included two aunts, Estelle and Rebecca Grable. Susan Rehkopf, archivist of the Episcopal Diocese of Missouri, recalls her father telling her she was baptized in the same font as Betty Grable. That font is still in use. Wags at the church call it the "Grable font."

Wherever it's best to remember Grable in St. Louis, part of her remained a South Sider long after she left the area for Hollywood. Pushed by her mother, Lillian Grable, Betty learned acting and dancing and started making vaudeville appearances. In the late 1920s, she moved with her mother to Hollywood. Her father, Conn, stayed behind, and Conn and Lillian eventually divorced. Betty appeared in her first film in 1929 and signed a contract with Samuel Goldwyn the next year. She was so popular that pinup pictures of her were carried by soldiers, sailors, and marines everywhere during World War II. Altogether, she acted in sixty-one films into the 1950s, including *Million Dollar Legs* in 1939 and *How to Marry a Millionaire* in 1953.

One of her last appearances was at the Muny Opera in 1971 in *This Is Show Business* with Don Ameche and Rudy Vallee. After she died of cancer two years later, an obituary in the *Post-Dispatch* said that when she returned to St. Louis in the 1930s to visit her father, she would stop by the home of her aunts at 4118 Juniata Street. "They have coffee every day, and there's sure to be something good to eat," she said. The two-story brick home still has a generous covered front porch and is down the street from Mann School.

JOE AND YOGI

It started with not-so-gentle games of King of the Hill in the 5400 block of Elizabeth Avenue. Mickey Garagiola and John Berra loved to stand at the top of the hill and push their little brothers Joe Garagiola and Lawrence Berra down. "We used to try to give them a hard time," said Mickey, who was Joe's big brother. Then Joe and Lawrence grew older, picked up bats and catcher's mitts, and became kings of a much bigger hill. Joe grew up to play baseball and be a Hall of Fame baseball broadcaster. Lawrence later became known as Yogi Berra, the Hall of Fame catcher for the Yankees and a well-known speaker of creative English. They lived across the street from each other. Ben Pucci, who played for the All-America Football Conference 1948 champion Cleveland Browns, was another of Joe and Yogi's neighbors and playmates on the block. Another Hall of Famer, broadcaster Jack Buck, later called the block home for a while, but when people on the Hill think about the great ones from Elizabeth Avenue, they're talking about Joe and Yogi.

When Joe and Yogi were little, Elizabeth Avenue was a great place for kids to play, and there was nothing they liked doing more than playing ball. "They were two peas in a pod," said Mickey, who died in 2010. Early on, Joe, Yogi, Ben, and others played for a team sponsored by the neighborhood's Stags Athletic Club. "They [Joe and Yogi] were the best ballplayers on the team, so you know they had to go somewhere," said teammate Charles Riva. Riva lived on the same block. Mickey wound up marrying Riva's sister Adele.

"There was always some-
thing going on, all the time,"
Riva said. Yogi painted
ten-yard lines on the street
during football season so
the gang could play touch
football. He dropped out of
school after eighth grade
to work at a factory, but
he was fired because he
would wander off at lunch
to play ball and forget to
come back to work. So he
played American Legion
ball instead. Mickey also quit

school after eighth grade to work as a waiter at the swank Ruggeri's Restaurant at 2300 Edwards Street. After Ruggeri's closed
in 1985, he spent the next fourteen years as a waiter at Pietro's
at 3801 Watson Road. He also gained fame locally from 1969 to
1985 by announcing on the old *Wrestling at the Chase* on KPLR
Channel 11. Never mind that he didn't go to high school. Everyone knew him for his class.

Joe was one person who didn't stop school at the end of
eighth grade. He played ball at St. Mary's High School and also
played for the old city WPA league. The Cardinals were so
impressed they gave him five hundred dollars to sign with the
team. The Redbirds also wanted to sign Yogi but wouldn't give
him the same five hundred dollar bonus. So Yogi went with the
Yankees. After Joe came to the majors in 1946, people on the Hill
celebrated by sponsoring Joe Garagiola Night at Sportsman's
Park. "It will always be a top thrill to me because that night I
saw many people there like Mama and Pop—people who didn't
know what baseball was but wanted to be there because 'this is
one of our boys,'" he said in his 1960 book, *Baseball Is a Funny
Game*. Garagiola spent nine years with the Cardinals, Pirates,

Cubs, and Giants before ending with a so-so .257 lifetime average in 1954. His career took off after that, first as a Cardinals broadcaster and then as an NBC baseball commentator and personality. Since then, he's stayed close to friends on the Hill and he used to call Mickey every Sunday.

Meanwhile, Yogi found glory as a catcher and a manager in both leagues. He became famous for sayings like "It's déjà vu all over again." That might lead people to think he's not too smart, but Mickey said it wasn't so. "He's not a dumb kid like they make him out to be," he said. Mickey's nephew Bruce Marren agrees. "He was never like that," said Marren, a freelance photographer and videographer who also lives in the 5400 block of Elizabeth and has seen Yogi from time to time. Yogi has friends and family here, including a niece who lives in the Berra house on Elizabeth. Marren has seen Joe Garagiola frequently through the years, including at the 2003 ceremony where his block received an honorary designation from the city as Hall of Fame Place. People on the block have welcomed those who come to see a place where so many famous athletes lived. "The neighbors are pretty friendly about tourists coming through," Marren said. During the 2009 All-Star Game here, "I thought about putting up a stand and selling photos," he said with a laugh.

THE SOUTH SIDE'S FOOT-STOMPIN', HOLY GHOST SINGIN', GOSPEL PLAYIN' DUO

On May 21, 1927, a doctor paid a call to deliver a baby in Datto, Arkansas. The boy's parents couldn't pay cash, so they gave him three dozen eggs and a red rooster. As the boy grew, he learned to give up his shoes every May 15 so they would stay in good shape for cold weather. As poor as he was, he found $7.50 when he was fourteen to buy a piano. Then Almus "Slim" Cox taught himself to play.

"I learned myself how to play that piano. I never had a lesson," Cox said one day in 2010, as he belted out a tune on an electric piano in a radio and recording studio in the back of his crowded Slim and Zella Mae Cox Furniture Store at 2831 Chippewa Street. He didn't mind that he never learned to read notes. It was more important that he play country gospel like his favorites, Jerry Lee Lewis, Jimmy Swaggart, and country gospel musician Howard Goodman. If he just read the notes in a service, everybody in church would fall asleep, said Cox, who died in 2012. "That's why Slim and Zella Mae can get up in those telethons and get the phones ringing," Slim said in the booming voice that watchers of the telethons and other programs on KNLC–Channel 24 knew so well. Slim's piano playing and the singing of his wife, Zella Mae, were familiar to viewers of KNLC, as well as seven low-power television stations and thirteen radio stations operated by Larry Rice's New Life Evangelistic Center.

The music was also familiar to listeners of Miroslaw Desperak's hillbilly country program on Catholic radio station FIAT 94.7 FM in Czestochowa, Poland. Slim and Zella Mae's song "Walking My Lord Up Calvary Hill" was one of the station's biggest hits at the start of 2010. Slim and Zella Mae recorded it in the 1960s, and it enjoyed a second life of sorts. It zoomed in popularity around the world in 2004 and again in 2010, where it raced up the worldwide country gospel chart. It was hot in Australia, Denmark, Canada, and England and in numerous states in the United States. "It makes me feel thrilled to know we're getting to people," Slim said. The Coxes also had their share of fans locally. "I love the old foot-stomping tongues of fire gospel," said Ridgley "Hounddog" Brown, who dropped in to Cox's furniture store one Saturday to say hello to Slim and Zella Mae. "He is a terrific piano player," said Brown, a retiree who did programming for KDHX 88.1 FM. "He plays it like a barrel house piano style."

Cox honed his style playing in bands and then with Zella Mae after they married in 1948. When she was born on October 23, 1930, in Mammoth Springs, Arkansas, her parents didn't have to give up three dozen eggs. Her father, a Pentecostal preacher, delivered her. Slim maintained he found out he really loved Zella Mae when he discovered she could pick 360 pounds of cotton a day. After they married, they sang on small radio stations in northern Arkansas and southern Missouri. They continued performing on the radio after he moved to Wellston in the late 1950s and worked for Schweig Engel Furniture. After twelve years at Schweig Engel, Cox started his furniture company on Chippewa. In the meantime, Slim and Zella Mae continued the musical work. In the morning before school, they recorded a fifteen-minute show at home. Cox then took the tape to KXEN Radio. They also recorded at least sixteen albums and went around the country on an old Greyhound bus. "It was very exciting and sometimes very tiring," said their daughter Sharon Hardcastle of O'Fallon, Missouri, recalling those days on the road. "I've been singing ever since I can remember." Another daughter, Brenda Chitty, also of O'Fallon, said, "It was like spinning in a circle around and around."

In later years, Slim and Zella Mae limited their performing to Larry Rice's radio and television stations, a radio show from 6 to 7 A.M. on Saturdays on WEW 770, and an annual performance at Kirkwood's Green Tree Festival in September. But they stayed active in the community. He was president of the Chippewa Broadway Business Association for seven years and was president of the Chippewa Neighborhood Association. "South St. Louis has been good to us," said Cox. He also credited his faith for what he had become. "We need to preach about a hell to shun and a heaven to gain," he said. It wasn't bad for somebody who cost his parents thirty-six eggs and a rooster.

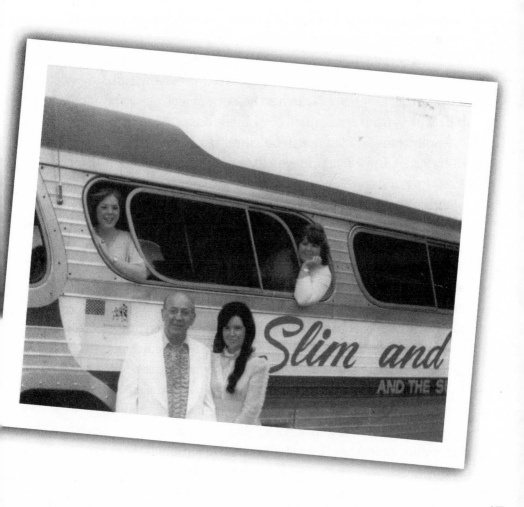

All of nine years old, Marshall E. McTague Jr. sat at Kiel Auditorium and heard Harry Truman belittle those who didn't think he had a chance in the 1948 presidential election. His father, Marshall E. McTague Sr., narrowly lost a bid for Congress four years before. In the 1950s, he'd be groomed to run for governor, but for now, he was one more person in the welcoming committee. "I remember Truman holding up the *Post-Dispatch* with scorn because they didn't endorse him," Marshall Jr. said. He also remembered shaking Harry's hand. Like his father, he went by Mickey. It was one of the first memories in a lifetime of collecting memories of important people he met.

Mickey related the story one Saturday afternoon in 2010 at Shaw Coffee at Marconi and Shaw Avenues on the Hill. He wore a dark green ivy cap, a herringbone jacket, a gray sweater, blue shirt, and green T-shirt. Over three hours, he spoke about the politicians and famous people he's known and worked for: Bob Hope, Lenny Bruce, Mayor Al Cervantes, Mayor Ray Tucker, Joe Garagiola, and Thomas Eagleton were on the list. He had pictures posing with many of them on the wall of his apartment at Donovan and Lansdowne Avenues in St. Louis Hills.

The year before he died in 2011, at the age of seventy-two, he spoke about how he lost his father at an early age. Three days after his son graduated from eighth grade, forty-seven-year-old Marshall E. McTague Sr. dropped dead of a heart attack. After that, Mickey's mother almost died of tuberculosis. Mickey took over as the titular leader of his family at 3128 Allen Avenue. Although the senior McTague had bought enough insurance to give his six children a good living, grief weighed heavily on Mickey.

The St. Mary's High School graduate, however, found a way out through comedy writing. As he moved into adulthood, big-name comedians started noticing. He wrote material for Lenny Bruce when he appeared one night in the mid-1960s

6501 Lansdowne Avenue
Saint Louis, Missouri 63109
(314) 752-9662

1971

Powell
Hall

Mickey McTague
Comedy Writer

at the Crystal Palace in Gaslight Square. Bruce gave him $200.
Garagiola gave him $250 for a monologue at the 1965 Baseball
Writers Dinner at the Jefferson Hotel downtown. But Mickey's
biggest connection was with Bob Hope. Mickey met Hope in
1958 when he was performing at the Muny Opera and wrote
topical material for the legendary comedian whenever he
was in the area. After Hope died at the age of 100 in 2003,

Mickey attended the private funeral Mass. An early check he received from Hope, for five hundred dollars, was to write some jokes for the Academy Awards in 1966. Over the years, he said he saw the change in comedy long enough to be able to make this observation: "Humor has become so mean-spirited, leaving almost nothing to the imagination, with a lot of spite in it." He might have gone elsewhere to be a big comedy writer, but he decided to stay on the South Side.

For most of his life, Mickey toiled for the city. He worked off and on for the city from 1959 to 1971, when he stayed on until he retired in 2007. By being in patronage jobs for the city collector of revenue, license collector, and sheriff's office, he was able to do work for mayors, including Ray Tucker and A. J. Cervantes. He was also close to Francis R. Slay, father of Mayor Francis G. Slay. Once in a while, he used to stop by the bar of the Eleventh Ward alderman, Albert "Red" Villa. He liked the cigar smoking of the legendary Seventh Ward alderman, Ray Leisure. He shared memories with the late Senator Thomas Eagleton and the late Governor Mel Carnahan. After he retired he worked on a screenplay about Bob Hope, Bing Crosby, and others coming back from the dead for a few days. The memories he shared of Hope are among the ones he collected in a lifetime of knowing countless people. Everybody knew Mickey McTague, because Mickey McTague knew everybody.

MAKING IT RIGHT
ON SOUTH KINGSHIGHWAY

The cop was aghast. A car dealer had asked for the keys to a customer's car so he could take it out and appraise it for a trade-in. As the story is told now, the dealer threw the keys up on his roof and told the customer he'd have to buy the car he was looking at or walk home. The customer went to the cop for help. When the cop demanded the keys back, the dealer said it was a civil matter and told him to stay out of it. The cop sent a paddy wagon around to pick up everybody at the dealership for stealing the keys. Word got around about what Officer Dave Sinclair had done at the North Side dealership, and the widespread practice stopped. Years later, when Sinclair's first dealerships opened on South Kingshighway early in 1966, he determined nothing like that would happen there. In the six years he operated on Kingshighway, he developed a reputation for honest dealings and hokey TV ads that made him a regional icon. In a business known for its crooks, when Sinclair died in 2009, everybody remembered him as the guy you told your grandmother to see about a car.

Sinclair started making that reputation in the midst of a crowded strip of auto stores. You could buy anything on South Kingshighway: Pontiac, Cadillac, Dodge, Lincoln, or Oldsmobile. In 1969, car dealers had twenty-one addresses from Southtown Famous north to Arsenal Street. They included such names as Vincel Pontiac, King Dodge, and Bender Best Lincoln Mercury. Add in McMahon Ford at Gravois Avenue and Chippewa Street and Placke Chevrolet and Christopher-Southwest Motor Sales Used Cars at Southwest Avenue and Kingshighway, and the number grew to an even two dozen. Sinclair had three of those addresses on either side of Tholozan Avenue on the east side of Kingshighway. Dave Sinclair Ford Used Cars was on the north side of Tholozan, and

Dave Sinclair Ford, Inc., and Dave Sinclair Ford Truck, Inc., were on the south side.

Dan Sinclair remembers those days. A lawyer and accountant who ran some of Sinclair's car dealerships, he's the oldest of Dave's seven children. "South Kingshighway was at the time the Manchester and South Lindbergh of now," Dan claimed. But he wasn't as impressed about the buildings and lots themselves. "It was small and old and antiquated." For all of this, Sinclair moved cars, in part with a familiar bet of a free undercoat if anybody beat his deals. He had been making this offer since he quit the city police in 1956 and started as a car salesman. By the mid-1960s, Ford offered to help set up Sinclair with his own business.

Not long after he opened, Dave Sinclair became a pioneer in local advertising by buying his own thirty-second spots on KPLR-TV Channel 11. "It was very primitive by today's standards," Dan said. The first one showed white-gloved hands on a black background dealing cards that said "For a great deal, come to Dave Sinclair." Later, he read his own copy behind a podium, as he did the rest of his life. People liked the ads, Dan said. "The customers felt like there was a personal emotional attachment. He was talking to *you*, not the masses of people. He was frequently quoted as saying he didn't want anybody to be unhappy that had done business with Dave Sinclair." And Dave didn't forget his roots. "He was a city policeman, and his father and uncles had been St. Louis city police officers," Dan said. "As soon as he got his own place, he started hiring ex–city policemen." Maybe forty or fifty city police officers eventually came to work for him. As an ex-cop, he kept his police revolver. He had it with him when he and others stayed overnight to catch a thief who'd been stealing cars from his lot. When the robber showed up, Sinclair used the revolver to keep him at bay until police came to take the crook away.

If Sinclair had gotten his wish, he would have stayed on Kingshighway. That's where his customers were, Dan said. But the place was too small. His used cars were stashed on lots for blocks around. "Ford Motor Co. convinced him to move. He did not want to move," his son said. Finally, he decided to move to 7466 South Lindbergh Boulevard. It's one of four dealerships the Sinclairs have today. The customers followed. Then as now, they knew if the car wasn't right, Dave Sinclair would make it right.

In hindsight, it probably wasn't a good idea, but then again, it did sell a lot of washers and dryers. As the cameras rolled at the Channel 11 studio, Steve Mizerany poured wood alcohol on top of a washer and set it on fire. "I was showing somebody it won't catch on fire," the master hawker remembered. But then some of the alcohol dripped down and caught some rubber on fire. Soon a backdrop curtain was ablaze. "The fire department had to come and put it out," Mizerany said. "It got a lot of play." For Mizerany, whose crazy antics and ads for his appliance stores were fixtures on local television stations from the 1950s until he retired in 1990, it was just another ad, and it all started on the South Side.

Mizerany died in 2011 at the age of eighty-seven. Before that, he got around in a wheelchair at the Bethesda Meadow skilled nursing community in Ellisville, but he was still eager to talk about how everything started with his father's grocery store at 10th Street and Park Avenue. He attended St. Vincent de Paul School not far from his house and then McKinley High School. Like everybody else in this Lebanese family, Mizerany helped out at the grocery store. Then his brother Joe started the first Mizerany appliance store at 3849 South Broadway after World War II. Friends and family helped out, including Joe Farhatt, a childhood buddy who would follow him through his career. Steve was out on the floor, hamming it up. "I always was a silly guy. I was sort of a nitwit," he said. He loved the Germans of South St. Louis. "They always bought from us," he said. "They're good people, the Germans." Soon, the Mizerany family opened a second store at 18th

THE DECENT BOYS

Street and Geyer Avenue. Then stores opened in Maplewood and Pine Lawn. Eventually, there were twenty-four such stores.

The ads were a big part of this increase. "I wasn't serious at all. It was 'act silly,'" Mizerany said. "Our commercials were so bad that the people liked 'em and bought." His son Vince explained the thinking this way: "The idea was to get people's attention on television." That got them into the store, where salesmen made the sale. He wasn't just silly on television, either. Vince said, "He was a riot to live with. Everywhere he went, he'd act silly."

Eventually, Farhatt and Steve broke away from others in the original Mizerany stores and formed Mizerany New Deal. In time, there were seven Mizerany New Deal stores, including one near the Bevo Mill at 4719 Gravois Avenue. And the ads continued. "His ad used to say, 'The Bevo Mill is next to us,'" said Bob Morris, a volunteer at Bethesda Meadow. To show Mizerany's prices were the lowest, he introduced a famous line, "Don't be confused. We don't bait and switch." He was on the radio with Jack Buck and worked with the famous announcer in the Celebrities Against Police softball fundraiser at Fox Park at Shenandoah and Ohio Avenues for the St. Louis Police Relief Association. The benefit raised about ten thousand dollars. He also became known for a routine in which he zoomed through his store on roller skates. These antics brought him considerable success. But, he said, "All that was an accident. It's not that I'm smart." Indeed, he succeeded in selling some people washers and dryers, but he made everybody laugh.

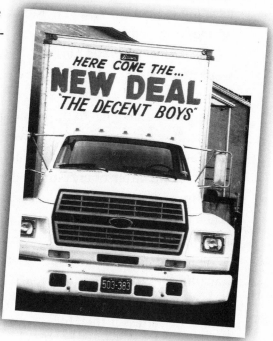

THE NIGHTMARES LINGER

The smile Sadik Kukic shows to customers of his Bevo Mill neighborhood restaurant conceals a darker reality. Too often, he awakens in a sweat. He's had another nightmare about the five months he spent in two Serbian concentration camps for the crime of being Muslim. He came from Bosnia to St. Louis in 1993 to escape an ethnic war following the breakup of Yugoslavia. About 250,000 people died and more than 3 million became refugees from 1992 to 1995. Tens of thousands of refugees like Kukic came to the South Side, bringing new vitality to an area centered in the Bevo Mill neighborhood. One of the earliest of those refugees, Kukic became a leader of the city's Bosnian community and the owner of one of the best Bosnian restaurants in St. Louis. He will often laugh about old times before the war with other Bosnians who come to his Taft Street Restaurant and Bar at 4457 Gravois Road, but the dreaded memories continue. If he's hiding the pain, he knows that many of his customers also are disguising anguish over what happened to them. "Some of us admit it. Some of us don't," Kukic said in his kitchen, while he prepared two rib-eye steaks.

For Kukic, who was born in 1965, the story began when he went to work for about seven years as a chef on boats traveling from the former Yugoslavia to Germany. Then the war broke out, and he came back to his hometown of Brezovo Polje in Bosnia. "I wasn't politically involved in anything," he said. One day, Serbs rounded up the men and brought them to a concentration camp. After twenty-three days, he was taken to another concentration camp, where he stayed for about four months. "They beat me, they didn't feed me, and I did what needed to be done," Kukic said. He weighed about 220 pounds when he came in and about 97 pounds when he left. "Every day there was different torture," Kukic said. "I was sleeping five months on a concrete floor. Sometimes they fed us, sometimes they didn't," he said. But then his old employer in Belgrade did a work of mercy. He said he needed the help of Kukic and fifteen others. "He was doing us a favor," Kukic said. "I can't forget him for the rest of my life." Kukic spent ten months working in Belgrade before the International Institute brought him to St. Louis along with his wife, Edina, his son, Emir, who is now twenty-one, and his brother, Ekrem.

Kukic was out of danger but still had to struggle. Broke and not knowing any English, he took a factory job and then a job at a taco place. "I didn't speak any English, and all recipes were in Spanish," he said. After he got a car in 1994, he moved up to a catering place and then to the St. Louis Club in Clayton. "Money was OK, but it was very good to have that kind of place on your resume," Kukic said. He learned English from his time in the kitchen, by studying at home, and six months of classes at the International Institute. In 2000, he opened his first restaurant, the Gulf Coast, at 3191 South Grand Boulevard. Then in 2002, he had a bout with cancer, which was cured when a kidney was removed. In March 2005, he opened Taft Street Restaurant and closed the Gulf Coast four months later. In four of the five years since then, the *Riverfront Times* has listed Taft Street Restaurant as the best Bosnian cuisine. Meanwhile, he served three years as president of the Bosnian Chamber of Commerce and was founder of the annual Bosnian Festival for the area.

He seemed the picture of the successful refugee immigrant, but his struggles continued. "Sometimes, these things come to you and leave you for a while," he said. But there are joys, including the time he spends with his daughter, Lajla, who is three. There is also his sense of thankfulness for being in America. "I consider St. Louis a good place to start for newcomers. And I deeply believe that the United States is a country of opportunity." Several years ago, heading back to the United States from a vacation trip to Bosnia, he thought, "We are coming home. We are coming home."

BUCKET JOE: HAPPILY OFF THE STREET

Like the stories of Wyatt Earp and Jesse James, the legend of Bucket Joe has grown over time, but Joe wasn't a lawman or an outlaw, only a homeless man on the South Side whom everybody seemed to know. He walked along Grand Boulevard and Gravois Avenue carrying a bucket he used to make money by washing windows. Some people remember him swinging at passing cars with an old broom at Chippewa Street and Gravois Avenue. Some yelled at Joe in derision, some in friendship. He hasn't been on the streets for years, and it would be easy to say somebody made up the stories about him, if it wasn't for the fact that so many people remember him.

Bucket Joe didn't disappear or simply go away; rather, he found a home. In an August 29, 1990, article, *South Side Journal* reporter Lois Kendall said Joseph "Bucket Joe" Mossberger had been living on the streets since he was eighteen in the early 1960s. "He lumbered up and down the sidewalks of the South Side for some thirty years, a big man with a shaved head and a loping gait. He wore raggedy dress pants chopped off at the knees and scuffed brogan shoes without socks. He rarely wore a jacket, except on the coldest days. And in either hand, he carried buckets." Home was an empty building or an alley. He ate what strangers fed him or what he found in garbage cans. "He'd been hit by cars, arrested by police and incarcerated in mental institutions," Kendall wrote. Then he disappeared, which led to speculation that something terrible had happened to him.

But Kendall had good news to report. He was living in a six-family flat on the South Side and receiving Social Security checks. He was sleeping in a real bed and eating regularly. He'd allowed a reporter to speak to him so those he had known on the street would know he was all right. Clifford Cockrell, a landlord and Forest Park Southeast resident, knew Mossberger all his life and was tired of seeing him on the streets. "He's very happy. He eats three meals a day," Cockrell said in

2010. Mossberger, who was developmentally disabled, hadn't had a drink in twenty years, Cockrell said. He had two cats and liked AM radio. He had a cake every birthday. Ever protective, Cockrell refused to allow another reporter to speak with Mossberger. Cockrell and Mossberger couldn't be located in 2014.

Most didn't know about this happy ending to a story that didn't start well, but speculation and memories remained, including in a public Facebook page. Don L. O'Toole Jr., who now lives in Louisiana, wrote on the Facebook page that he made friends with Joe as a youngster selling newspapers in front of the White Castle at Grand and Gravois. "He was the source of lots of fun and dare I say entertainment," he wrote. "Hopefully, he is doing as well as he was when this article came out," O'Toole said in 2010. Others who wrote on the page recalled hearing that he got the name "Bucket Joe" because he carried a beer bucket around. Another remembered giving Joe a gallon of Kool-Aid when he was playing roller hockey behind the Oak Hill School at Morgan Ford Road and Osceola Street one summer. One more recounted how Mossberger wandered into Mass late at St. Mary Magdalen, 4611 Sutherland Avenue, when the priest was finishing giving out communion. He wandered up to the front and waited until the priest came back down and served him communion. Mossberger left, and the priest never mentioned it again.

Many of the senior citizens at the Five Star Senior Center at 2832 Arsenal Street had plenty of memories of Bucket Joe. "I remember seeing him walk up and down the Gravois-Grand area carrying his white milk jug," said Mike Howard, who managed the center. Doloras Morfia, one of the senior citizens at the center, recalled that Mossberger ate sometimes at a feeding program at St. Vincent de Paul Church, 1408 South 10th Street. "I've heard stories that he was all right, that he moved into an apartment," said Billy Watkins, another senior citizen at Five Star. At the clubhouse of the Gateway Corkball Club on Walsh Street east of Ulena Avenue, Marty Kirner recalled seeing Mossberger years earlier at Amberg Field in the Dutchtown neighborhood. "He'd walk all over South St. Louis. He was homeless before homeless was popular," Kirner said. Everybody saw him and everybody realized the need, but thanks to one person who decided to fill that need, Mossberger came off the streets.

HOLDING COURT AT A BAR

Alderman Albert "Red" Villa didn't bother meeting constituents in a fancy office at city hall. He didn't even have a fancy office in his Eleventh Ward, which covers most of the Carondelet neighborhood at the southern end of the city. A constituent who wanted a job, a pothole fixed, or trash picked up headed to Table No. 1 at the Cottage, a saloon Villa operated at 8129 South Broadway. The complaint would be resolved over a cold Bud, while Red puffed away at his ever-present stogie. Several times a week, Villa headed to city hall to take care of the problems he'd discussed at the Cottage. That was the way it was with Villa, who remarked that his political base was his saloon.

Villa operated the saloon from 1931 to 1977. For two years before the end of Prohibition, the saloon technically wasn't legal. He co-owned two taverns before he purchased the Cottage with fellow politician Jimmy McAteer. Twice during Prohibition he was convicted of misdemeanor bootlegging violations.

After he was elected to the Board of Aldermen in 1953, Villa was known for being a gentleman and for always working for his constituents. He didn't always go along with others on the board. He once refused to take a twenty-five-hundred-dollar-a-year raise and chose instead to use the money for lights at baseball fields in Carondelet Park. That didn't mean things always went smoothly for him. In 1967, he quit the board to avoid a suit brought by the circuit attorney's office because he lived outside the ward at 3841 Holly Hills Boulevard, in the Thirteenth Ward. By the time he resigned, he had moved into the Eleventh Ward, to 510 Dover Place. The Board of Aldermen quickly voted to reinstate Villa. He put a sign in front of his house that stated, "Red Villa Lives Here."

Villa lived to see his son Thomas serve in the state legislature from 1974 to 1984 and then be elected president of the Board of Aldermen in 1987. Red was thrilled to see his son pound the gavel at meetings. But it didn't last. Red died of cancer on December 7, 1990, at his home on Dover Place. He had lived long enough to see the Board of Aldermen name its chamber after him and a bust of him holding a cigar dedicated at Virginia Avenue at Ivory Street.

Thomas made an unsuccessful run for mayor in 1993 and served as aldermanic president until 1995. He later served another tenure on the state legislature, from 2001 to 2009. At the Board of Aldermen, though, there wasn't a Villa for two years after 1995. But in 1997, Matt Villa, Tom's nephew and Red's grandson, was elected alderman in the Eleventh Ward. Matt resigned in 2011 to watch the family lighting business, and his uncle replaced him. As in all but two of the past sixty-three years, a Villa is listening to constituents' complaints, in the Eleventh Ward, but not always at a table in a bar.

Alderman Albert (Red) Villa

A devoted public servant to the City of St. Louis and especially dedicated to the · Carondelet Community and the 11th Ward

DEDICATED 1990

A HARD LESSON IN POLITICS

Just twenty-four years old, law student James Shrewsbury didn't realize what he was getting into when he volunteered for the re-election campaign of State Representative Ed Bushmeyer before the 1980 Democratic primary. The St. Louis Hills resident knew Bushmeyer's opponents would get ugly. He knew the Seventh Ward Democratic Organization of Sorkis Webbe Sr. and Alderman Sorkis Webbe Jr. had a reputation for stealing votes by collecting absentee ballots but only mailing the ones for their candidates to election officials. The Webbes were prepared to do it again for Robert Brandhorst, their candidate for Bushmeyer's Eighty-Third District state representative seat in the near South Side.

Bushmeyer, Shrewsbury, and other volunteers knew the only way to counter this duplicity was to arrive at the doors of people after they'd received an absentee ballot in the mail and before one of Webbe's people showed up to collect them. That way, they could receive an absentee ballot, notarize it, and mail it to election authorities. Shrewsbury apparently crossed a line when he notarized absentee ballots at the Webbe Senior Citizens Home, 1020 South 14th Street. The home was named for former state senator Anthony Webbe, a cousin of Sorkis Webbe Sr. The senior Webbe told two underlings—Norm Clark and Pat Gandy—to take care of Shrewsbury.

On the Friday before election day, Shrewsbury was struck in the back of the head with a blackjack as he left the Webbe Senior Citizens Home. He fell flat on his face and would have been struck again if a woman with him hadn't screamed. Shrewsbury was hospitalized for four days, suffering from a concussion, bruises, and cuts. It took him months to get back on his feet, but there were no permanent injuries. Bushmeyer narrowly won in regular voting but lost after absentee ballots were added.

What happened didn't deter Shrewsbury from being in politics, but it taught him a lesson. "I learned there are some people who will do anything to win an election," Shrewsbury said. In

Punch #31

Jim
Shrewsbury

Your Attentive and Aggressive Alderman

Endorsed by

St. Louis Globe-Democrat

ST. LOUIS POST-DISPATCH

Hubert H. Humphrey Young Democrats

The Shrewsbury Committee   6201 Devonshire Ave. St. Louis, Missouri 63109   353-5690
John H. Wieder, III, Treasurer

time, the Webbes, Gandy, Clark, and two others were indicted for mail fraud, voter fraud, obstruction of justice, and violation of civil rights for their role in the 1980 election. The civil rights violation was for Shrewsbury's beating. The senior Webbe died before the trial, but others were found guilty or pleaded guilty.

In 1983, Shrewsbury went on to be elected alderman from the Sixteenth Ward, which includes the St. Louis Hills neighborhood. From 2001 until 2007, he was president of the St. Louis Board of Aldermen. Thus, for six years, the person holding one of the most powerful jobs in the city had a sharp memory of what a club on his head meant to silence political opposition. Shrewsbury believes instances of outright violence have declined in St. Louis politics, but this student in the school of hard knocks believes corruption remains strong among politicians.

At lunchtime at the start of the 1980s, Slay's Restaurant at 2652 Hampton Avenue was one of the favorite hangouts of local politicians. The owners were Anthony and Francis R. Slay, whose family had been influential in the city Democratic Party since the 1930s. Francis R., who operated another Slay's Restaurant in Grantwood, had been state representative and city recorder of deeds. He still was Democratic committeeman in southwest St. Louis's Twenty-Third Ward. Anthony was the kind of person who knew everybody who came to the restaurant, St. Louis city comptroller Paul M. Berra told the *St. Louis Post-Dispatch*. On slow nights, Anthony would take sandwiches over to a police station nearby and talk with police officers. "He was well-liked and always had a cigar in his mouth," Berra said.

People thought the restaurant's location next to a police station protected it from crime, but it didn't help Anthony when he came to the restaurant the morning of Sunday, March 28, 1982, to unlock the door to let workers in and start work for the lunch crowd. Bobby Hines, a porter, arrived at 9:25 A.M. and found Slay bleeding heavily from the head. He was semiconscious on a chair in the dining room splattered with blood. Blood covered the floor in the kitchen and hallway. A large quantity of meat was gone from the cooler, and a company car was missing. An ambulance rushed Anthony to a hospital, where he died of extensive brain injuries at 12:20 P.M.

Early the next morning, the stolen car was found in North St. Louis. Inside was the billy club used to kill Slay. Byron

Restaurate

Follins, who had been dismissed from his job as a porter and busboy at the restaurant, was arrested and charged with capital murder and stealing the meat. At Follins's trial, two restaurant employees said Follins had asked for their help in setting up a robbery at Slay's. Follins testified he hid in a crawl space over a walk-in freezer all day on March 27 and waited until workers left at 2 A.M. He claimed he put large amounts of meat into bags and drank beer and smoked marijuana while he waited for Slay to arrive. He wanted to use Slay's automobile to take the meat away, he said. He testified he wanted to knock out Slay, not kill him. The jury didn't believe him. They found Follins guilty of taking the meat and beating Slay to death. In April 1983, he was sentenced to fifty years in prison without parole.

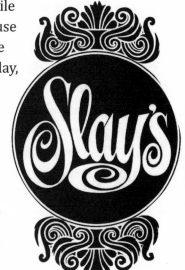

Two years later, Francis R. Slay's son, Francis G. Slay, was elected alderman in the Twenty-Third Ward. He was elected Board of Aldermen president in 1995 and mayor in 2001. As the nephew of Anthony Slay, the mayor can say with so many other city residents that he is a close relative of a murder victim.

SINCE 1911

Anthony Slay Fatally Beaten

A DECADE OF FEAR

In the spring of 1992, a series of hideous crimes shook the South Side. For years after that, women in St. Louis Hills, Southampton, Tower Grove South, and elsewhere didn't quite feel safe walking outside. It began on April 1, 1992, when a fifty-two-year-old woman was raped in her home near Nottingham Avenue and South Kingshighway Boulevard. On April 3, a thirty-two-year-old woman was raped in her home around Chippewa Street and January Avenue. Then, on April 20, a man pressed a butter knife to the throat of a seventy-five-year-old woman in her home near Morgan Ford Road. Then he raped her. Another sexual assault followed on May 9 in a home near Hampton and Loughborough Avenues.

Other rapes followed, and police stepped up their investigation of someone called the "South Side Rapist." At Francis Park, women jogged in groups. Police set up a phone line for people to call in information. Women stayed home at night, kept their windows locked, and installed new door locks. As time went on the rapist moved out of the South Side. He moved to Collinsville, Illinois, in 1994, then Arnold and St. Charles in 1995, and South St. Louis County in 1996. Police kept up their pressure against the rapist, but he stayed at large. In May 1997, about 150 people who packed the basement of St. James the Greater Catholic School in Dogtown listened as police told them to stay alert. Soon after, Police Chief Ron Henderson acknowledged police were stumped. An FBI profile suggested the rapist was clean-cut and knew the area where he struck. The rapes continued.

In October 1998 police got the break that would identify the rapist. A city detective obtained a saliva swab of Dennis N. Rabbitt, forty-two, of Cedar Hill while the policeman was investigating a report that someone was looking into windows on Alma Avenue. On November 6, the test confirmed Rabbitt indeed was the South Side Rapist. He'd been married and had a bar downtown. Those acquainted with this man, who had spent much of his life in St. Louis, said he was the last person they would have thought would have committed such crimes. Using the evidence, authorities in Jefferson County charged Rabbitt with the rape of an eighteen-year-old woman. Rabbitt, who had lived much of his life in South St. Louis, disappeared. Then prosecutors in St. Louis charged Rabbitt with forty criminal counts in eleven rapes.

Meanwhile, a nationwide manhunt was underway, including items in *America's Most Wanted*. After three months, two Albuquerque, New Mexico, police officers arrested Rabbitt at a motel as they looked for a fifteen-year-old runaway. The girl was unharmed. Rabbitt was brought back to St. Louis. In January 2000, he pleaded guilty to forty-nine counts of sexual assault on fourteen women from 1988 to 1997. So ended a decade of terror for women on the South Side. Authorities said Rabbitt may have committed more than one hundred rapes, many in the South Side. He is serving six consecutive life sentences, which means he'll never get out of jail.

THE MURDERING DENTIST

By day, Dr. Glennon E. Engleman fixed the teeth of patients in an office on Gravois Avenue near the Bevo Mill. By night, he had a darker side. It seemed to be a case of Dr. Jekyll and Mr. Hyde when police in 1980 got a capital murder warrant charging Engleman and another man with shooting to death Peter J. Halm of Kirkwood in 1976. Friends and people who ran businesses near his office said this was not the man they knew. But it soon became clear that his warmth and friendliness were sometime things.

It wasn't the first time police suspected Engleman of murder. The dentist was called in for questioning when James S. Bullock was gunned down with a .22 caliber pistol near the St. Louis Art Museum in 1958. At the time, Engleman's ex-wife had been married to Bullock for six months. Engleman insisted he was innocent of any wrongdoing, and police couldn't pin anything on him. Five years later, police also suspected Engleman of killing Eric L. Frey of Clayton, who worked at a drag strip Engleman owned in Pacific. Frey died in an explosion while he tried to blow up a well in 1963. The death was ruled accidental, but authorities still speculated.

Thirteen years later came the incident that would lead to the first charges against Engleman: the fatal shooting of Peter J. Halm in 1976. It took four years for authorities to file charges against Engleman. Then Halm's wife, Carmen Miranda Halm, gave authorities the information they needed. She was a dental assistant for Engleman when he urged her to marry someone who could be murdered for insurance money. Soon after that, police moved to charge him in the car bombing that killed Sophie Marie Barrera on January 14, 1980. She had died in an explosion as she started her car outside her dental lab near the South Side National Bank. She had sued Engleman for failing to pay bills he owed the lab.

After the explosion, Ruth Engleman, one of the dentist's ex-wives, went to federal authorities. They put a wire on her and sent her back to Engleman to draw him out. In those conversations, Engleman admitted killing Barrera and said he had worked with Carmen Miranda Halm and had received ten thousand dollars from her brother after killing Halm. In his federal trial in the killing of Halm, prosecutors submitted testimony from an informant that Engleman had admitted killing Frey in 1963 for insurance purposes and dividing the proceeds with his widow.

In separate trials, Engleman was found guilty in the killings of Halm and Barrera and was given two life sentences. In prison, he pleaded guilty to the heinous murder of Arthur and Vernon Gusewelle in 1977 and their son, Ron Gusewelle, in 1979. The target in the murders of the three Edwardsville, Illinois, residents was the senior Gusewelle's half-million-dollar estate. Ron's wife, Barbara Gusewelle Boyle, was released from prison on parole in Illinois after serving half of a fifty-year sentence for murdering her husband.

Altogether, Engleman was a suspect in a dozen killings. He died at the age of seventy-one in 1999 at the Jefferson City Correctional Center. The murdering dentist was gone, but hardly forgotten.

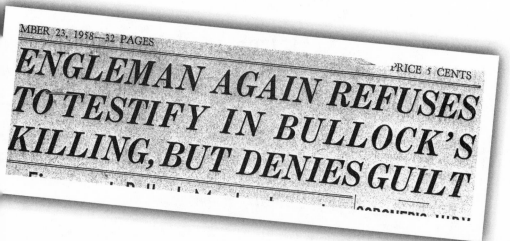

MBER 23, 1958—32 PAGES

PRICE 5 CENTS

ENGLEMAN AGAIN REFUSES TO TESTIFY IN BULLOCK'S KILLING, BUT DENIES GUILT

Albert T. Jefferson had every reason to be angry at white people. As the son of ex-slaves, he surely heard story after story about injustices done by slave masters. But he spoke gratefully about the sacrifices that many whites had made for African Americans. In his own community of Carondelet, white churches stepped in to prevent a lender from foreclosing on the mortgage of a historic African American church, Corinthian Baptist Church, 6326 Colorado Avenue. And he noted that white citizens of Carondelet financed Dred Scott's appeal to the Supreme Court for freedom. Those included Roswell Field, father of poet Eugene Field, and William T. Blow, father of Susan Blow, who started the first public kindergarten at the old Des Peres School

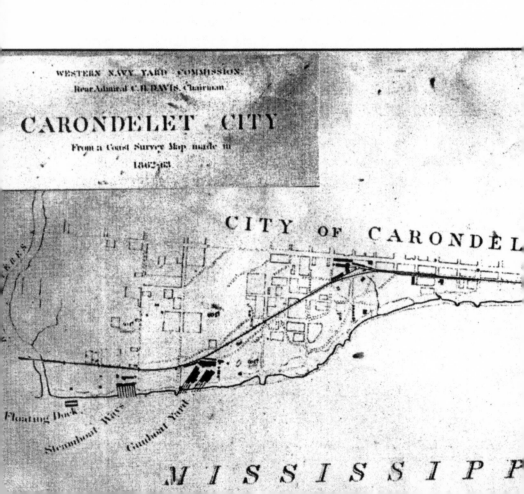

WESTERN NAVY YARD COMMISSION.
Rear Admiral C. H. DAVIS, Chairman.

CARONDELET CITY

From a Coast Survey Map made in
1862-63.

CITY OF CARONDEL

Floating Dock

Steamboat Ways

Gunboat Yard

MISSISSIPP

in Carondelet. William Blow also donated land for the first African American church in Carondelet. He is said to have given the land for Public School #6 (later Delaney School), the community's school for African Americans.

Jefferson's family had come to Carondelet after the Civil War to work on a farm north of Jefferson Barracks. Jefferson was born in 1899 in the family home at 7010 Minnesota Avenue, and lived his life there as a bachelor. He attended the Delaney School and then Sumner High School on the city's North Side. It took him ninety minutes riding three streetcars to reach Sumner, the only city high school for African Americans. In 1919, he took a job as a letter carrier, a job he kept all his life. An article in the old *Bugle* newspaper on December 1, 1979, recounted how Jefferson long had studied the area's black history and was still active in the Carondelet Historical Society. He died in 1989.

Jefferson lived in a community that included African Americans long before other parts of the South Side. As early as 1850, the census counted twenty-six slaves and twenty-six African American freedmen who worked as farmers, draymen, and servants. After the Civil War, blacks impoverished by the collapse of the plantations started moving in to find work in the community's steel mills and blast furnaces. They also worked on river packets and boats clearing the Mississippi of logs and debris. The population grew to about 450 in 1880, 600 in 1890, about 850 in 1900, and about 1,063 in 1910. The 2000 census said there were 1,847 African Americans in Carondelet out of a total population of 9,960.

A list assembled by Jefferson showed African Americans living in Carondelet had a variety of professions. African Americans who lived in Carondelet included Virginia McKnight, administrator of Homer G. Phillips Hospital; Albert Burgess, a lawyer and prosecutor; John R. Steele, superintendent of buildings at Jefferson Barracks; and Hugh White Jr., a lawyer who went on to be elected to the Missouri legislature. Lu Lu Tour (Lucille H. Schwartz), a newspaper columnist, came from Carondelet, as did Clark Terry, a musician on the staff of the Columbia Broadcasting System. Other African Americans included firefighters, police officers, doctors, a dentist, and numerous teachers. For spiritual sustenance, most attended Corinthian Baptist Church and Quinn Chapel African Methodist Episcopal Church, 227 Bowen Street. Both remain active. Jefferson believed that whites had helped these and other institutions for African Americans, but he still recognized and fought injustice. He picketed the old American Theater in St. Louis for segregating blacks in the second balcony and fought the barring of African Americans from Cardinals and Browns baseball games, downtown restaurants, and other gathering places. But he was positive about his own community. "Race relations have always been good in Carondelet," he once wrote.

PLACES

Above a glass counter filled with doughnuts of every kind are pictures of Superman in a bright blue outfit next to Superman memorabilia. On another wall are photos of a guy dressed up like Superman. Blown-up copies of comic strips are posted and a model of a skeleton in an old barber's chair is near a display window of the store at 1618 South Broadway in the Soulard neighborhood. Behind the counter of John's Donuts, Alice Parris waits on customers seeking their sugar in the form of a glazed doughnut or one stuffed with jelly. These aren't the hours-old doughnuts on display at convenience stores or supermarkets, but freshly-fried just a few feet away.

Nearby, John Pearcy sits at a table covered with newspapers. "When I was about 18, my father told me, 'What other business can you be at where you make so many people happy?'" At age 14, he started helping his dad at Pearcy's Pastry Shop in Metropolis, Illinois. The connection with a town with the same name as Superman's adopted home city explains the presence of all the Superman stuff in the shop, while the shop Pearcy's father ran explains why John Pearcy has been in the business all his life.

Pearcy opened the shop on April 1, 1982. He thought of the connection with April Fools' Day after his first day receipts were $35. But business picked up, and steady customers ensured his business would remain strong. Those include Gary Craig, a retired high school and college English teacher who lives in the South Side's Gate District. He's been coming since the late 1980s. "I shouldn't be eating them, but once in a while, I decide I'm going to get a doughnut," Craig said, sitting at a table next to a window, wearing a black beret and a blue cardigan sweater. At another table, Don Griffith offered his own appraisal. "The atmosphere, charisma, nostalgia of the place makes it very comfortable," said Griffith, who had been coming in for two and a half months during breaks from a job nearby. "It's not just the icing, it's the dough itself."

The continued health of John's Donuts is one of many proofs that convenience stores, supermarkets, and chain stores have a way to go before they replace old-fashioned mom-and-pop donut shops on the South Side. At 5120 Southwest Avenue on the Hill, they throng to O'Fashion Donuts Inc. At Loughborough and Hampton Avenues, they get their treats at a free-standing store, painted green, with the name St. Louis Hills Donut Shop.

Near the Missouri Botanical Garden, the chosen address for apple fritters and jelly doughnuts is 1904 Vandeventer Avenue. That address—1904—is the same as the year the St. Louis World's Fair opened. Hence the name "World's Fair Donuts." "My father-in-law opened it one year before we bought it from him," said Peggy Clanton, who has owned the shop with her husband, Terry Clanton, since 1976. The two work at the shop seven days a week. Their son comes in five days a week from Potosi to help. The family doesn't mind the work. "You don't look at it that way. We look at it as a service to our customers," Peggy Clanton said. Their customers keep coming back to buy apple fritters, cake doughnuts, glazed doughnuts, and so many other kinds of sweet things. "Some of 'em I see two or three times a day," she said.

They include sixty-year-old Freeman Daigle, who has been coming to World's Fair Donuts since he was a kid. Now sixty and a North St. Louis County resident, he's been bringing in his nephew Aaron Hines since he was a baby. Hines is now nineteen and a resident of west St. Louis County, but loves coming back for doughnuts whenever he can.

Customer satisfaction is one factor noted by Kay Schwarz, the part-owner of the Donut Drive-In at 6525 Chippewa St. It's been in business since 1953, long enough for the owners to get to know what people like. "The neighborhood really supports it," Schwarz said. "These are all hand-made." One customer who stopped by said he came for his kids. "We stop here sometimes once a week for my little girls to get a sprinkle doughnut," he said. "They're very friendly. Their doughnuts are outstanding," said another customer.

Eddie Strickland baked at the Donut Drive-In until 2007. That's when he opened Eddie's Southtown Donuts at 4701 South Kingshighway Boulevard. As the boss does at all such places, he works long hours. But he doesn't mind. He loves the customers. "Everybody's humble, likable, laughable, joke-able," he said, smiling. In a week, about six hundred dozen doughnuts go out the shop's doors, but at a cost. "You see how my back hurts now," Strickland said. It's nothing that a good glazed doughnut couldn't fix.

Considering how much space Anheuser-Busch got from putting up the building at 4527 Virginia Avenue, the brewery may have paid too much for it. It lavished its cash on an ornate three-sided, two-and-a-half-story Tudor Revival structure, with glazed green brick on the outside and stucco and timber on the inside, reminiscent of an inn in Bavaria. But after spending all that money, the company only had enough space on each floor for a small apartment. But that's only if the point is to put up a cheap building with a lot more than space. "Only Anheuser-Busch could have spent that kind of money on a small building in 1910," noted Anthony Duncan, the architect who now owns the building that long was known as the Stork Inn. It opened as a neighborhood stucco and timber biergarten restaurant, but it was much more than that. The brewery meant it as an advertisement. "In architectural terms, they were putting together an edifice," said Duncan, who operates his architectural business on the first floor. The root of the word *edifice* is *edify*. Before TV and Facebook, companies often used their buildings for advertising.

Construction came as the cry for Prohibition of alcohol increased throughout the country. Anheuser-Busch asked the architectural firm of Klipstein and Rathmann to build a restaurant and tavern that would show drinking in moderation at its best. It was the first of eleven the brewery erected to burnish the image of drinking as a respectable family activity, according to a National Register of Historic Places application penned by architectural historians Karen Baxter and Esley Hamilton and research associate Timothy P. Malone. The application was successful. The most well-known of the eleven were the Gretchen Inn (now Al Smith's Feasting Fox Restaurant) and the Bevo Mill. Anheuser-Busch had in mind the image of the bringer of the babies when it named the tavern on Virginia Avenue the Stork Inn. The intent was to promote a product for expectant and

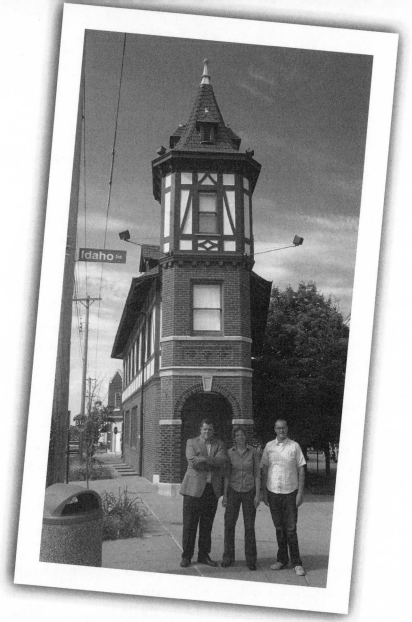

nursing mothers called Malt-Nutrine. But there may have been more to the story than that. On the second floor was a reception room and dance hall. The third floor was an apartment for those who ran the bar. Except for the sidewalk, the 29-by-64-by-70-foot building occupied all of the triangle surrounded by Virginia, Taft, and Idaho Avenues. The shape was the result of street grids from the once-separate towns of St. Louis and Carondelet coming together at that point, Duncan said. At the narrow point where Idaho and Virginia met, horses refreshed themselves at a trough.

The coming of Prohibition seemed to show the brewery's campaign as a failure, but only for a while. With the end of that experiment in 1933, the Stork Inn again became a popular neighborhood tavern. Duncan hears the history of the building from men in their eighties who stop by. Often, they'll say they were sent out by their fathers to bring home a pail of beer. "It was always a pail," Duncan said. "They couldn't spill it or they were punished."

The tavern closed in the early 1990s and quickly went into disrepair. Pigeons had free reign on the inside. Then came two saviors, Gwyn and Dale Preston, owner of Preston Art Glass. They bought the building for $15,000 and restored it for $150,000. They converted the second and third floors into an apartment and opened the Stork Inn Creamery and Ices Shop at the corner of Idaho and Virginia. Lovers of ice cream and shaved ice bought their treats at a door at the narrow corner. Duncan, his wife, and their three sons lived nearby at Bellerive Boulevard and Vermont Avenue. He often looked at the place when he drove by.

The desire for independence caused Duncan to take more than a passing interest in the building. After working for Hellmuth Obata Kassabaum, he decided it was time to go into business for himself in 2005. That year, the building was mostly empty. So he bought it and moved his firm into the first floor. He kept the apartments, but closed the ice cream shop. He needed the space for his architectural business, and he didn't want to sell ice cream.

"As an architect, I don't need a lot of parking. I need a small space for architects and myself," Duncan said. He loves the way the building shapes into two street grids. "I'm just pleased that somebody owns it that can take care of it and use it."

A ROYALE BAR ON THE HIGHWAY OF KINGS

Want a daiquiri with the taste of the South Side? Try the Holly Hills Daiquri from the Thirteenth Ward. How about an old-fashioned reminiscent of the South Side German? The Bevo Old-Fashioned from the Fourteenth Ward is for you. And you'll find no better sidecar cocktail than the Lafayette Sidecar from the Sixth Ward. Those and other drinks from the city's twenty-eight wards are ready for serving at the Royale on South Kingshighway Boulevard, just south of Arsenal Street.

The names of the drinks offer one indication that the Royale is not your typical South Side neighborhood bar. It's a popular hangout for Democratic leaders like Missouri Governor Jay Nixon and U.S. Senator Claire McCaskill and for a group of Young Democrats who meet there.

During the 2008 presidential election, bar owner Steve Smith plastered the second floor outside wall of his building with a twelve-by-eighteen display of Shepard Fairey's Hope/Progress/Change portraits featuring three identical pictures of Barack Obama in different colors. Others, like Missouri Republican Party Chairman Ed Martin, also stop by, just to add zest to the conversation. Smith admits, though, that the number of Republicans who come is limited. "Some Republicans I think feel unnecessarily hostile to the place," he said.

But it's not just for political talk that people stop by. A runners' group meets at the Royale early every Tuesday night before making its rounds around the neighborhood. When they're done, members return to commiserate and drink half-price Schlafly beer on tap. Bicyclists like the place. So do librarians who like to come by for Dewey Decimal drinks. It's pretty much what Smith had in mind when he bought the Real Bar in the mid-2000s and rechristened it the Royale. The name came partly from Rue de Roi, the old name for Kingshighway, and partly from the fact that he's owned a couple of Delta 88 Royales.

Only forty-one, Smith already has nearly thirty years in the bar business. "At thirteen, I started washing dishes in a basement bar in Webster Groves," said Smith, who was born in Chicago and grew up in Kirkwood and the South Side. "My sister worked there, so I guess they turned a blind eye to it," he said. "My father had bartended from time to time, and my mother was a stewardess, so we have that service in our blood." He went on to graduate from St. Louis University High School in 1991 and to receive his bachelor's degree in history from St. Louis University in 1996. Outside of school, he did events for the *Riverfront Times* and the City Museum. He worked for KDHX radio and as a portable vendor at Busch Stadium and Wrigley Field. In 2002, he opened a boxing gym on North Broadway called the Panda Athletic Club. He cashed in staging "Hoosier Weight Fights."

In 2005, he started the Royale. "There was a clear demand for a place like this in the neighborhood and in South St. Louis," Smith said. The crowds both on the inside and the back seating can include young folks, older folks, families, even kids drinking soda next to their parents. "I try to make as many people feel as comfortable as possible." He says he'd like to have a place where mom would like to hang out.

The Royale has played host to signature parties for such things as the Kentucky Derby, complete with derby hats, spring dresses, and mint juleps. In a Cuban missile crisis party, people dressed as if it was 1962 and the world was about to end. It included duck and cover drills. Just before the August 2014 primary, it hosted a debate on a proposed transportation sales tax increase.

Smith is happy with the way the Royale has turned out. "I wanted to have a place in the classic sense of the public house," he said. "When you connect with your neighbors, you might be able to find a job, find a place to live." He thought there was a clear demand for such a place, and he was right. "For the size of the place, we do a tremendous amount of business," Smith said. As for the political stuff, he said, George Washington planned the Revolutionary War in a tavern.

YOU WANT STUFF? GLOBE DRUGS'S GOT STUFF LIKE YOU WOULDN'T BELIEVE

Readers of the *South Side Journal* in 1989 could always count on seeing full-page ads with dozens of unbeatable deals that shouted "buy me." For a crisp dollar bill, anyone could walk out of Globe Drugs with three 3.53-ounce cans of Brunswick sardines, all swimming in tomato sauce. A quart of Bondex Ready Mix Concrete and Mortar Patch was on sale for $2.98, marked down from $3.49. For everyone who bought a package of Doxidan laxative and stool softener for $1.79, the store would throw in a second pack of this most important item for free. At one time, bargains like that pulled customers to Globe Drugs locations at 2626 Cherokee, 2700 Cherokee, Spruce and Tucker Boulevard, 9335 Gravois Road in Affton, and 1900 South Broadway. After the store at 2626 Cherokee closed in 2010, only one Globe Drugs location remains, at 1900 South Broadway. Around the same time the store at 2626 Cherokee closed, the final location dropped its pharmacy. But the selection of discounts and closeouts still is as unpredictable as ever.

For a mere $3.98, one day in July 2014, a customer could walk away with a 6.3-pound institutional size can of green beans. Diabetic socks sold for $1.98 a pair. Four single-serving bowls of Special K were a cool $1. A budding musician could buy a guitar for $29.95. The deals keep customer Doug Wolf coming back around twice a week. He gushed at the variety of merchandise like coffee, candy, chocolate, and liquor, but admitted that he spends more than he should. "I love the store, because it's unique," said Wolf, who lives in Belleville, Illinois. He stops by Globe Drugs while driving to assignments as a computer technician for IBM. "I bought a barrel with a palm tree sticking out of it," Wolf said. But his wife isn't impressed. "She thinks I'm a hoarder."

In the company's seventy-fifth year, the man in charge at Globe Drugs is Sandy Cohen. "We try to get a nice variety in here," said Cohen, a sixty-seven-year-old pharmacist. The first store opened on Broadway about a half-block north of the current one. "Globe Drug got its start back in 1939 when the Cohen boys—Al, Abe, Joe, Is, Julius, Louis, and Bernard—decided to open a business that was more than just a drugstore," the Globe Drugs website brags. "They grew up in the Depression and understood the true meaning of a dollar, so they wanted their customers to have an affordable and convenient shopping experience." Cohen's dad, Joe, was a pharmacist, as were two other

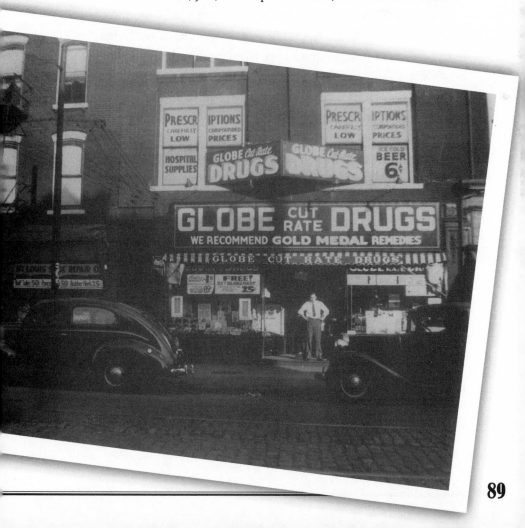

brothers. Sisters and others in the family also helped. An old picture shows Cohen's dad standing in front of the first Broadway store. "This area down here was a New York type of neighborhood," Cohen said. "The wives worked, the brothers-in-law, the sisters-in-law." A customer who asked to talk to Mr. Cohen might wind up speaking to anybody in the store.

Sandy Cohen never worked for anyone else. An early helper was Rick Ruzicka. Now fifty-seven, he's Cohen's trusted assistant. Ruzicka goes to buying shows to pick out the just-right selection of discounted and closeout stuff for Globe Drugs's shelves. Among the treasures Ruzicka has carted back are John Kerry bobbleheads, packs of 1990 baseball cards, a Jamaican CD, all kinds of—er—valuable merchandise. Several of the items are put in boxes, gift wrapped, and sold for $1.98 as surprise packages. "You never know what could be in it," Cohen said. In the old days, things that didn't sell went into the packages. Now Ruzicka looks for it when he goes to shows.

KTRS radio personalities Martin Kilcoyne and Andy Strickland loved the surprise packages so much that they excitedly opened one on the radio. They moved in the tradition of such media people as former *Post-Dispatch* columnist Elaine Viets, who often wrote about the store's offbeat selection. Wines fill numerous shelves, and Globe Drugs is known for its own brand of coffees and mounds of chocolate candies made in the store's basement. One bit of equipment in the store can melt eight hundred pounds of chocolate at a time for such treats as heavenly hash and pecan caramel turtles. Other stores may be feeling the pinch of Walmart or the Internet, but Cohen says he's doing fine. Maybe it's that it fills a niche no other store can. "We hear all the time, 'You just don't see stores like this any more,'" Cohen said. There's always something to buy, and when customers can't decide, they can always choose the surprise package.

HARRY BRINKOP GUESSES RIGHT

The time and place seemed all wrong. But in the depths of the Great Depression, Harry Brinkop emptied the bank to bet on a South Side spot for a new shopping center. He came up all aces. "A real estate man, like his father before him, he put his finger down on the map at the intersection of a couple of streets where the deep ruts meandered off south and west between yellow clay hills to nowhere in particular," *Post-Dispatch* real estate editor Virgil G. Baker wrote in 1947.

The unpaved streets Brinkop chose when he started his Boulevard Frontage Company in 1930 were Chippewa Street and Hampton Avenue. Some might have doubted Brinkop's wisdom when his first building opened at the end of December 1939. But today, Hampton Village Plaza remains vibrant. Farther west, the empty shell of what was once the Crestwood Plaza/Mall/Court stands as example number one of how many shopping centers blossomed after World War II, only to wither later. But cars still pack the parking lot at Hampton Village Plaza as they have for seventy-five years.

When the economy still hadn't recovered from the effects of the Depression, Brinkop looked ahead to a happier time, when mom, dad, and the kids would pile into their cars and head off shopping. But he knew he had to act quickly if he didn't want to lose the chance to assemble his shopping center. Although most of the land he wanted was undeveloped, much of it already had been subdivided for homes. The Great Depression helped him. Baker wrote that a developer had purchased seventeen lots for bungalows in the area of what is now the main square of Hampton Village. The developer refused to sell for seven years but finally gave up in 1937 because of problems with other business projects. Brinkop finished buying land for the center in 1938.

More good news would follow. City residents passed a bond issue calling for the widening and paving of Chippewa and Hampton. The state provided more money to pave Hampton, Chippewa, and nearby Sulphur Avenue, as did the federal Depression-era Works Progress Administration. And the state transferred its all-important Route 66 designation from Manchester Avenue to Chippewa. It guaranteed Chippewa would be a main auto route.

So it was that the *Globe-Democrat* reported on February 6, 1939, about plans for a $7 million shopping center with a series of Williamsburg Colonial style buildings with space for about two hundred businesses. There would be a parking lot capable of holding about three thousand automobiles. Brinkop boldly predicted the cars would come from such prosperous nearby communities as Webster Groves, Lindenwood, Shrewsbury, Affton, Glendale, Southampton, and Holly Hills.

On August 1, 1939, construction began on the first store, the air-conditioned 20,000-square-foot Hampton Village Market. It was a good sign when fifteen merchants signed up to operate thirty-three stalls, but a bad omen when the market opened in the middle of a blizzard on December 14, 1939. Business was lousy, and rents went unpaid. An effort by area businesses to take over the lease on the market failed. That allowed the popular Bettendorfs grocery chain to move in and rename it Bettendorfs Village Market. Shoppers flocked to the market until October 1970, when Schnucks took it over. After Schnucks closed the store in 1989, the National supermarkets built another store in the center in 1993, only to see Schnucks acquire it when it took over the chain in 1995.

After the war, Brinkop filled in the center with offices and stores. In 1948, J.C. Penney signed a twenty-year lease to be an anchor store. Today, it's as popular as when it opened. Brinkop opened more colonial-style store and office buildings on the west side of Hampton and the north side of Chippewa. A discount store opened on the west side of Hampton in the 1960s. Today a Target store occupies that space.

In the 1970s, historian Norbury L. Wayman wrote that Hampton Village was probably the oldest shopping center in Missouri. "It was unique because it consisted of a single building with off-street parking around the store," he wrote in a history of city neighborhoods now on the St. Louis city website. "A considerable part of this involves drive-in business which has been created by the phenomenal increase in automotive use since the war. " Today, the DESCO Group operates the nearly 230,000-square-foot center as Hampton Village Plaza. Only five of the forty slots, representing less than 10,000 square feet, are vacant. The center remains within a prosperous driving area. Three quarters of a century after the Hampton Village Plaza opened, it is still showing that Harry Brinkop guessed right.

The method seems simple enough. Each week, coat eight tons of fresh chicken with a mix of flour, milk, and eggs. Fry and serve to happy customers who keep coming back, week after week. It's a recipe that has kept things clucking at Hodak's for more than fifty years. "The fresh chicken, freshly breaded, is really what makes it stand out," said Rick Kuehn who started waiting tables and bartending at the restaurant and now is its unofficial historian.

Although he freely disclosed the three ingredients of the coating, Kuehn's not about to give the amounts or anything else about the mix. That's a secret. One of the early ingredients of the mix is no longer available. But it's pretty close to what customers first tasted when Tony Hodak and his wife, Helen, opened the restaurant more than fifty years ago. Hodak's opened at its present location at 2100 Gravois Avenue in 1962. Previously, Tony operated another restaurant with a relative of his wife. At one time, Hodak's was one of four Gravois Road chicken restaurants that also included Medich's, Lemmon's, and

Mary's Fine Foods, Kuehn said. "We're the only ones remaining," he said. Ralph and Charlene Hegel bought the place in 1989. Ralph is mostly retired, and Charlene is now in charge. "They're wonderful people. That's why so many of us have worked for them for so long," Kuehn said.

"It's always been a working man's kind of place, a family kind of place," Kuehn said. "It's not unusual to have anything from judges to laborers." About half are regulars. As many as 240 hungry customers can sit in the restaurant at a time, not to mention another 100 in a banquet room. To serve them, a semi-tractor-trailer full of fresh chicken from Jones Poultry in central Illinois pulls up to the door at 6 A.M. five days a week. Crinkle-cut french fries fill a whole cooler. Hodak's buys about a ton of cabbage a week for slaw. Although fried chicken is the favorite, Hodak's offers a complete menu, including fried fish. Fried cod and jack salmon are big sellers on Fridays.

All this makes Hodak's major palate pleasers for Robert Laske and Rita Dodson. The two, who are both eighty-two, met in 1950 and got engaged before Laske went into the army. But their paths took them elsewhere, although they've spent much of their lives on the South Side. They reconnected in their eighties after Laske's wife died. Hodak's is a favorite place to catch up with each other. Laske's been coming since 1965, and Dodson since 1972. "The service is good. The food's good. They give you plenty, and it's reasonable," Laske said. Plus, one of their favorite waitresses is also Dodson's granddaughter. Melissa Smith started at Hodak's in 1994 at the age of fifteen. She's been around long enough to know many of the regulars by name. "It's like home, you know, that's the thing, like they say, welcome home." And what better thing to eat at home than chicken fried with a secret coating?

THE SOUTH SIDE'S LAST MOUND

When Sue Maehl moved to a new house in 1963, she knew it was on top of an Indian mound, but she wasn't sure of the significance. She searched for Indian arrowheads but didn't find any. The house's location near the Mississippi River seemed more interesting. Being atop a forty-foot mound, the view was spectacular. Maehl has learned much more about that mound and its importance since she got married and moved away in 1969.

The Sugarloaf Mound is the last of about forty mounds that once dotted the city of St. Louis. Located at 4420 Ohio Avenue, it's the only one that wasn't leveled to make way for development in what was once known as the Mound City. Sugarloaf was created as a part of the vast network of mounds that Mississippians created on both sides of the river from 1050 to 1400. Cahokia Mounds in Illinois has received the most attention, care, and study, but Sugarloaf Mound will have its day.

After Maehl and her two brothers moved out, their parents, Walter and Eileen Strosnider, remained. They refused to allow anyone to dig on the property, but they allowed it to be nominated to the National Register of Historic Places. The designation the mound received was important for the Strosniders, because they wanted their property preserved. They maintained that concern when they put the land up for sale in 2008. So the family was delighted when a group of concerned citizens, including U.S. Representative Russ Carnahan, contacted the Osage Nation Indian tribe in Oklahoma. The Osage Nation bought the mound in 2009. It wants to raise money to remove the houses, put fences around the property, and make it part of an educational center about the importance of the Sugarloaf Mound and other mounds. "We're thrilled. We were very happy to sell it to the Osage Indians," said Maehl, a retired schoolteacher living in California. Before her father died in June 2009, he learned the Osage Indians were interested in buying the property. He was glad they would preserve it. Her mother, who is still living, also was pleased. "She saw a lot of the articles in the paper about it. She was very impressed that where she had lived had been an important place."

The Osage Nation bought the mound because of the role they believe it played in their own history. Although their tribe is based in Pawhuska, Oklahoma, people in the Osage Nation believe their ancestors likely were among the Indians who built the Cahokia Mounds and the mounds in St. Louis. Andrea Hunter, the tribal historic preservation officer, said that early immigration stories indicate that the Osage and other tribes came down the Ohio River and then up the Mississippi to St. Louis. In addition, archaeological and anthropological evidence indicates that the social structures, rituals, games, and other practices of the Osage and the builders of the mounds were similar, she said. All this makes it likely that the Osage played an important part in the building of the mounds, she said. But Bill Iseminger, assistant manager of the Cahokia Mounds State Historic Site, offers a note of caution. It's not totally clear yet, Iseminger said. "In their oral tradition, they believe they were here some time in the past," he said. "They feel a connection to the mounds in the area. There's very little archaeological evidence that either proves or disproves it." However, Hunter is convinced of the importance of preserving the Sugarloaf Mound. "Hundreds of years of our people's past were erased from the landscape in the wake of the urbanization of St. Louis," Hunter said. "There isn't anything that we can do to bring back what has happened, what was so mindlessly destroyed, but we certainly can impact what happens at Sugarloaf today."

HOW CAVES MADE BEER KING

In the nineteenth century, the South Side's underground was like Swiss cheese. "Two hundred fifty years ago, St. Louis would have been a sinkhole heaven," cave explorer Joe Light said. He is president of the Meramec Valley Grotto, a chapter of the National Speleological Society that meets in the St. Louis area. Indeed, in their 1996 book, *Lost Caves of St. Louis: A History of the City's Forgotten Caves*, Charlotte Rother and Hubert E. Rother Jr. listed fifteen caves on the South Side. The reason is the mix of fairly thick limestone and dolomite bedrock formations underground in Missouri. In time, groundwater dissolves it. The vegetation, climate, and rainfall all work together to add carbonic acid to the groundwater, allowing it to dissolve minerals.

The city's nineteenth-century brewers may not have known why the caves were there, but they recognized opportunity in them. With the onset of lager beer, brewers needed a cool place to store and ferment their product, and caves fit the bill. Caves helped establish the brewing industry in St. Louis as much as thirsty German immigrants. Adam Lemp was among the biggest South Side brewers who used caves. In the early 1840s, Lemp started using a large system of caves on the road to Carondelet, now South Broadway. He first brought his beer to the caves from his brewery on Second Street, between Walnut and Elm Street, but in 1850, he built a brewery right over the cave. Another brewery, the Minnehaha, also operated briefly nearby in the same network of caves. Prohibition brought an end to Lemp's empire, but the vast buildings of his brewery are still at Cherokee Street and South Broadway.

English Cave, which is almost entirely under Benton Park, southeast of Jefferson Avenue and Arsenal Street, is another cave used by a brewery. It was first used by Isaac McHose and Ezra English of the St. Louis Brewery in the 1840s to store their beer. Then they used it as a place to sell their product.

Renamed Mammoth Cave and Park, the place offered relief from the St. Louis heat in the summer and the cold in the winter. They tried vocalists, balloon ascensions, and hiring a military band to entertain the crowds, but nothing could keep Mammoth Cave from closing. A project to store wine there was short-lived. Using English Cave to grow mushrooms also failed, but the mushroom venture was a success at a cave at Keokuk Street and California Avenue. A *Post-Dispatch* article in 1898 reported a company was growing an average of sixty pounds of mushrooms a day in the cave.

In the 1950s, Lee Hess opened the caves formerly used by the Lemp and Minnehaha Breweries to the public. Hess was a pharmaceutical manufacturer who bought land above the Minnehaha part of the cave along with the old Chatillon-DeMenil Mansion and grounds in the 1940s. He wanted to make money by having tourists visit the Lemp and Minnehaha caves. He tore down tenements and erected a museum that he intended as an entrance to the cave. As workmen made their way down, they found numerous bones. Curious, Hess sent samples to the American Museum of Natural History in New York. Geologists for the museum analyzed them and determined they were fossils of peccaries: hairy, tusked, pig-like animals that died in a prehistoric flood of the Mississippi. Hess opened Cherokee Cave in 1950 and closed it when the Missouri Highway Department bought the cave, the museum building, and the historic Chatillon-DeMenil Mansion in 1961 to make way for Interstate 55. The Landmarks Association persuaded the state to move the path east, so it didn't affect the mansion. The association then got Union Electric (now Ameren) to put up the money to buy the historic home. As for Cherokee Cave and so many other caves under the South Side, they were sealed and filled in. They've been clogged and filled in by construction projects, rubbish, or other means, but they're evidence of the fact that an accident of nature helped make beer king on the South Side.

As floodwaters from the River des Peres began to recede early on August 21, 1915, authorities made an awful discovery in a one-room cabin at 1720 January Avenue just south of Manchester Avenue. They found the bodies of David and Adeleine Bowman, their daughter Ruth, son John, and granddaughter Bessie Westmoreland. Six more bodies were found about a mile west in the suburb of Ellendale, just beyond the city limits. They were killed by a normally tranquil stream that swelled to a mile wide as nine inches of rain brought by a tropical gulf storm fell in twenty-four hours on August 20–21. Altogether, 11 died and 1,025 people lost their homes. The hundreds rescued included Anna and E. G. Stange, who lived at 3600 West Primm Street, on the west side of the river south of the present route of Interstate 55. With the river rising in their home, E. G. Stange chopped holes first in the attic and then through the roof. They were on the roof for six hours before they were rescued.

The deluge—the latest and worst of five since 1897—convinced St. Louisans something had to be done to tame this little waterway that so often became a beast. Before the floodwaters had receded, Mayor Henry W. Kiel was discussing a bond issue to make the River des Peres safe. The next year, the City Plan Commission adopted a plan that included running the river underground from the city limits through Forest Park to Macklind Avenue and an open channel from Macklind to the Mississippi River. The plan also proposed running a scenic boulevard next to the river from McCausland Avenue to the Mississippi. City residents agreed on the need. In 1923, they approved an $11 million bond issue for River des Peres flood work, as part of an overall package of $87.4 million to finance improvements for the city. Workers spent the next nine years completing the River des Peres Sewerage and Drainage Works.

As many as forty-five hundred workers were kept busy doing more work on the River des Peres as part of the Depression-era Works Progress Administration. In the six miles from Pernod Avenue to the Mississippi, WPA workers installed the white stones on the side and concrete on the bottom so familiar to residents of the area today. They also created the four-mile-long River des Peres Parkway south of Lansdowne Avenue. While the work represented an improvement, for decades people complained about the stench from the river caused by improper drainage of sanitary sewerage into the waterway.

Then, in 1971, a coalition of several organizations proposed converting the six miles of the River des Peres above the Mississippi into a waterway navigable by small craft. The idea, perfect for wags who talk about the "River des Peres Yacht Club," also envisioned boating, fishing, bicycle and jogging paths, small parks, and dams and reservoirs to control water in the riverbed. The backers also suggested putting ice on the riverbed for ice skating during the winter and keeping part of the riverbed dry in the summer for fairs or art shows. Most of the plan didn't go anywhere, but today a bike path called the River des Peres Greenway runs along the river from Lansdowne to Interstate 55. It's part of a plan by the Great Rivers Greenway to create six hundred miles of bike paths around the area. Although some may rightly call the River des Peres ugly, it's clear that work done since the 1915 flood has made it a much safer waterway.

Behind displays of organically grown spinach, fresh cilantro, onions, potatoes, and dozens of other homegrown organic vegetables, Arlene Kruse spoke about the evils of buying processed foods from the supermarket. "Women don't care anymore. They buy in small amounts. Their tastes have changed in the fact that they don't know what good food tastes like," Kruse said. She sells the antidote in the Soulard Farmers Market stand of Kruse Gardens of Columbia, Illinois. She started the stand in the late 1980s and has been to the market for all of her seventy-three years. Other Kruses before her had stands in Soulard. "My grandmother used to talk about coming here. So did my mother," she said above the din of the crowd.

In fact, people have been coming to Soulard Market since 1838, when Julia Cerre Soulard donated land for use as a public market. She specified that if the property wasn't used as a public marketplace, it had to be returned to her heirs. The sign at the market claims that it began in 1779, but even the market's website acknowledges that's a myth. In 1779, St. Louis was a trading post nearly a mile away, and Soulard Market is considered the city's third public market. It is, however, the longest continually running market in Missouri, and one of the oldest in the country.

In the 1840s, a one-story building went up on the site. A second floor with a large meeting room was built in 1865. The 1896 tornado heavily damaged the building. It was repaired without the meeting room. In 1929, a new $267,000 structure replaced the old building and sheds. Its two-block-long design mirrored the Brunelleschi Foundling Hospital built around 1419 in Florence, Italy. There was room for all vendors to stay inside and a central second floor with a gym and all-purpose room. Twenty thousand people turned out for the dedication of the market on May 8, 1929.

The market stayed busy. In 1950, journalist Jim Fox wrote about it in the old *Star-Times*. "Corn from Columbia, cabbage from Commission Row and beans from Barnhart—these are but a few of the commodities for sale

at bustling Soulard Market, a city institution which dates back to the early nineteenth century," Fox wrote. "Today, as in earlier days, Soulard is called a farmers' market, with many of the hucksters bringing in their wares from nearby communities. Customers come from north and south St. Louis, the East Side, the county, and, of course, the Soulard neighborhood."

Today, people are still coming, and not just for the freshest and the cheapest produce around. With nearly ninety vendors, the market offers much more than produce, including spices, meats, collectibles, breads, and even pets. Scott Androff, who works at Boeing during the week, sells his photos at the market on Saturdays. His display includes a black and white picture of someone getting into a Volkswagen behind his apartment in Soulard in 1973, color pictures of the old and new Busch Stadium, the Venice Café in Soulard, and the old Coral Court Motel. Androff started serious photography after high praise from his family. Then on New Year's Day in 1998 he made a resolution to help the market. That was the beginning of his stand. He enjoys it, but it doesn't make enough to go full-time. Another vendor, Matt Leitch, contends the secret is persistence. "Bad times get balanced out by the good times, we hope," said Leitch, of Richmond Heights, who sells incense and fragrance oil. In good times or bad, everything at the market keeps people coming back.

The Chatillon-DeMenil Mansion has had several lives, each enough to attract visitors. Built in 1849 and expanded in 1861, the house at 3352 DeMenil Place is one of the finest surviving examples in the Midwest of the brick Southern Greek Revival homes that once filled the city, and it was once a landmark for Mississippi riverboat pilots.

The house was built by Henri Chatillon and his wife, Odile Delor Lux, both of whom had lived in Carondelet, five miles south of St. Louis. She was the granddaughter of Clement Delor de Treget, who founded Carondelet in 1771. Through his contacts in St. Louis, Chatillon met Francis Parkman, an explorer who immortalized Henri in the book *The Oregon Trail*. "His bravery was as much celebrated in the mountains as his skill in hunting; but it is characteristic of him that in a country where the rifle is the chief arbiter between man and man, he was very seldom involved in quarrels," Parkman wrote of Chatillon. A painting showing Chatillon with his first wife, an Indian squaw named Bear Robe, the daughter of the Oglala Sioux chief Bull Bear, hangs on the mansion's wall. She died in the mid-1840s, before he married Odile Delor Lux in 1848.

The Chatillons kept the house until 1856, when they sold it to the French physician Nicholas DeMenil and Eugene Miltenberger. DeMenil's grandfather had renounced his 1,100-year-old title during the French Revolution. Nonetheless, Nicholas DeMenil still was of noble descent when he came to America on a tour. While in the New World, he fell in love with Emilie Sophie Chouteau, granddaughter of Auguste Chouteau, a founder of St. Louis. Soon they were married. In St. Louis, Nicholas owned several drugstores and was a real estate broker. The DeMenils bought Miltenberger's share of the home in 1861 and used it as a summer retreat. DeMenil built an addition with columns and a portico. He then leased part of his land to men who wanted to start a brewery. When they couldn't pay their debts, he seized the brewery in 1867. He also built a row of homes and stores east of his home but discovered too late that the new construction ruined the view of the river. DeMenil died in 1882, and his son Alexander inherited the house.

Alexander was an attorney, literary critic, and poet. One poem defended his great-great grandmother Marie Therese Chouteau against criticism over her affair with St. Louis founder Pierre Laclede. In 1902, he took part with Mark Twain in the dedication of the steamboat *Mark Twain*. Alexander was a member of the board of the 1904 World's Fair, which explains why the mansion currently displays a large collection of fair memorabilia. Alexander died in 1928, and the mansion was maintained but not occupied.

In 1945, the family sold the home to pharmaceutical manufacturer Lee Hess. He and his wife lived in an apartment upstairs while he built a museum and made nearby caves into a tourist attraction. Cherokee Cave opened in 1950 and closed in 1961. By that time, the Missouri Highway Commission had chosen a path for the new Interstate 55 that took it through the DeMenil Mansion. Pressed by the Landmarks Association of St. Louis, the state later moved the route east but took Hess's property, including the mansion. The Landmarks Association stepped in to save the mansion. The state agreed to sell it to the association. Union Electric (now Ameren) put up the money for the house's purchase, while a campaign began to raise money for renovations. In a ceremony on May 16, 1965, the Landmarks Association transferred the building to the Chatillon-DeMenil House Foundation. Today's museum is a fitting memorial to the eclectic variety of people who called the mansion home.

City Hospital was destroyed by a fire and a tornado. It had been so overcrowded that there was nowhere to put desperately ill patients. It survived wars and depressions for nearly 140 years. Yet it couldn't survive tight budgets, a decline in patients, and the political climate of the 1980s. The story of that hospital began in July 1845, when the St. Louis City Council passed an ordinance appointing a committee to choose a site and develop plans for a hospital to serve the indigent. That committee selected the present intersection of 14th Street and Lafayette Avenue. In June 1846, less than a year later, the hospital received its first patients. It was just in time for the cholera epidemic of 1849 that killed a tenth of the city's population. But less than ten years later, in May 1856, a fire razed the young city hospital. Everybody got out except an insane man who ran back in after being rescued. The next year, a new building was in place to receive the sick again, but it wasn't long before the hospital was overwhelmed. In August 1870, the hospital's supervisor gave the Board of Health a report that twenty patients were turned away in just one day because of a lack of space. Two years later, the Board of Health called the hospital a "disgrace to St. Louis" and announced an effort to build a new hospital to house at least 750 patients. The existing facility was always overcrowded, and doctors often had to turn away extremely sick patients.

One wing of the new hospital had been completed by May 27, 1896, when the hospital was destroyed by a massive tornado that killed 255 people. While the city waited for a new hospital, patients were housed at the newly named Emergency Hospital 1, the Convent of the House of the Good Shepherd, in the block surrounded by 17th, 18th, Pine, and Chestnut Streets. Soon the ruins of the old hospital became an eyesore. The *Post-Dispatch* remarked on May 28, 1897, a year and a day after the tornado, that while nearby Lafayette Park looked as pretty as ever, the hospital was even more of a wreck than the day after the storm. Meanwhile, loud critiques were heard about the condition of Emergency Hospital 1. Mayor Henry Ziegenhein promised action, but it wasn't until 1905 or 1907, depending on the sources, when a new hospital opened. Eventually, eighteen buildings in the Georgian Revival style would fill the ten-acre City Hospital site at 14th and Lafayette.

The history of City Hospital in the twentieth century was influenced by racial politics. The city opened its first hospital for African Americans in 1919, City Hospital No. 1, at Garrison and Lawton Avenues, in the old Barnes Hospital. Then, in 1937, Homer G. Phillips Hospital opened at 2601 Whittier Street, named after a man who fought for its construction but was murdered before the building was completed. A system with one North Side hospital and one South Side hospital worked fine until the 1970s, when it became clear the city couldn't afford both. Those on the North Side fought suggestions about closing Homer G. Phillips. But in 1979, Mayor James Conway closed it.

This helped lead to Conway's defeat in the 1981 mayoral election. His opponent, Alderman Vincent C. Schoemehl promised he'd reopen Homer G. Phillips if he won. After he won, Schoemehl saw ballot measures needed to fulfill his promise go down in defeat. He gave up on reopening Phillips. Meanwhile, low patient counts and City Hospital's aging buildings were making it hard to keep that facility open. Black aldermen fought the idea of closing the last place in the city where the poor could be treated, but on June 22, 1985, Schoemehl announced City Hospital patients would be moved to Charter Hospital at 5535 Delmar Boulevard. Within little more than a week, one patient remained to be moved: mobster Paul Leisure. He'd been kept in the hospital's prison ward awaiting trial on murder charges. The county joined the city in creating the new St. Louis Regional Medical Center at 5535 Delmar Boulevard. It didn't last, and the indigent were left to find medical care in clogged emergency rooms.

In the years that followed, efforts to reuse the empty buildings on the City Hospital property were largely unsuccessful. By the late 1990s, windows were gone. From the streets, trees could be seen growing out of the building. Mattresses and personal items could be seen tucked into corners, signs that the homeless had moved in. But the abandoned hospital came to life again in the mid-2000s when a company led by Chris Goodson and Trace Shaughnessy developed 102 condominiums on six floors of one building facing Lafayette Avenue. More is planned for what is now called the Georgian. As with so many formerly abandoned places on the South Side, new life is coming to the old City Hospital.

THE ASYLUM ON ARSENAL STREET

In August 1911, the area was shocked to learn how forty-year-old Eva Jarvoubek, a patient at the City Sanitarium, was choked to death by a straitjacket she was wearing. The outcry was loud about what happened at the city's institution for the mentally ill. Dr. C. G. Chaddock, a member of the City Hospital visiting staff, told the State House Special Investigations Committee that the use of mechanical contrivances for quieting violent patients was wrong. Attendants too often used straitjackets and similar restraints when they should use humane care, he said. It was a brief moment of light for the institution inside a tall red-brick domed building on a hill at 5400 Arsenal Street. After this incident, things went back to normal. The asylum once again became that looming building visible on the horizon throughout the South Side, where people wondered what went on inside. The asylum's history was a mix of mistreatment and sincere efforts to help mentally ill people, always limited by a lack of funding. Instances of mistreatment have declined in recent years as effective medical treatments for mental illness have become known, but increasing limits in state funding have harmed efforts to improve the lives of mentally ill people at what is now known as the St. Louis Psychiatric Rehabilitation Center.

The institution first opened as the St. Louis County Lunatic Asylum on April 23, 1869. The building went up in the country, full of fresh air thought to help mental illness, said Barbara Anderson, who was volunteer director of the hospital from 1988 to 2006. The building itself was designed to bring that air inside. But in fact, treatment of any sort was wanting. "It was basically warehousing people with mental illnesses," Anderson said. "There was no clinical criteria by which someone measured another as being psychologically disoriented." Sometimes women were brought in suffering from postpartum depression and often ended up institutionalized for years. "It was a way to get rid of your wife and run around with some young girl," Anderson said. Patients also could have been alcoholics or suffering from syphilitic dementia, or just plain poor.

Treatment was cruel at worst and misguided at best. In the basement, some patients were placed in six-to-eight-foot-wide cubicles with straw on the floors. "People would defecate on the floor, and they would sweep it out every day," Anderson said. "It was cold and damp down there, and people slept on the floors." Those patients were usually African American, or whites who were out of control. Upstairs, patients would be treated to all the amenities of the Victorian household, including reading rooms and pool rooms. These rooms also were thought to improve patients' mental health. To shock them into sanity, people were placed in vats of ice cold water. "They did the best they could, based on the incredible ignorance they had," Anderson said.

As time went on, the institution's name changed to the St. Louis City Insane Asylum and then the City Sanitarium. When the city sold it to the state for one dollar in 1948, it became the St. Louis State Hospital. In 1997, it moved to new quarters on the same property at 5300 Arsenal Street and became the St. Louis Psychiatric Rehabilitation Center. The domed building at 5400 Arsenal became an office building for the Missouri Institute of Mental Health and the State Department of Mental Health.

Through the years, as the building's name changed, one ineffective therapy replaced another. Patients danced, were given beauty treatments, and sang operettas. A newspaper ran a feature story about how straps, straitjackets, and manacles were replaced by outdoor recreation and occupational therapy, but other articles told of cramped and unsanitary conditions. Nothing really helped, though, until the discovery of medications that treated mental illness.

However, here and elsewhere, their promise was limited when patients were released without enough of a structure to treat them in the community. Today, people continue to see the big building with the green dome on Arsenal Street wherever they go on the South Side. What they may not see is how budget cuts are still hurting patients.

THE GOLDEN DAYS OF CHEROKEE STREET

A good way to start a conversation with a septuagenarian or an octogenarian from the South Side is to ask about Cherokee Street way back when. He or she will quickly start talking about the excitement of the place, how busy it was, and how it was possible to go there and buy anything worth having. Indeed, in the 1940s and 1950s, Cherokee Street was the place to shop for people who didn't want to go downtown. There was a bit of Bedford Falls from *It's a Wonderful Life* in Cherokee Street.

The housewife who opened her *South Side Journal* on January 3, 1952, would find ads from at least a dozen Cherokee Street stores. One of them, Fairchild's Department Store, offered quilted lined jackets for $8.88 in its January store-wide sale. J.C. Penney was selling Cannon towels for sixty-seven cents in its white goods sale. At Morris Variety, you could buy two boxes of Kleenex for twenty-five cents.

If that housewife brought her husband to Cherokee Street that cold Friday night, they would find more than one hundred businesses in the six blocks of Cherokee Street from Jefferson Avenue west to Nebraska Avenue. They would see more than a dozen places to buy clothes, at least ten places to buy shoes, and at least seven jewelers. They would pass stores named Woolworth, S.S. Kresge, Western Auto, 905, and Walgreens. If they wished, they could buy a hat, a drink, a burger, a washing machine, a can of paint, or a sewing machine. Had they come during the day, they could have bought fresh-baked bread, brought in a suit to be cleaned, picked up a dozen roses, deposited a paycheck, gone to a doctor, or had their eyes examined. But since it was Friday night, they would have to settle for watching a movie at the Cinderella or going dancing at the Casa Loma.

Within a few years, Crestwood Plaza, South County Center, and other malls opened, drawing shoppers away with them. The city's population dropped. Neighborhood shoe stores, department stores, and movie theaters disappeared. Any septuagenarian or octogenarian will say it never will be the way it was. But that's not bad. People may buy their jewelry someplace else, but there are attractions on Cherokee Street that people there sixty years ago couldn't have experienced. On a spring Saturday afternoon, people fill the outside tables of the Mexican restaurant La Vallesana at 2801 Cherokee Street. The sound of Mexican music and people speaking Spanish is heard often on the street. For those who speak English, there's the Black Bear Bakery at 2639 Cherokee Street and Foam Coffee & Beer, 3359 South Jefferson Avenue. To the east is Antique Row, which people in the 1950s didn't have. The old times are gone, but each generation knows its own pleasures.

In the earliest years of St. Louis, much of the land south and west of the city was set off as common fields, communal land used for farming and grazing. By 1836, civic leaders moved toward selling this land. The boundaries of that common land were present-day Grand Boulevard on the west, Park Avenue on the north, about six blocks east of Jefferson Avenue on the east, and Delor Street on the south. The idea of organizing and naming the streets was noble—name the east-west streets for Indians or Indian tribes and the north-south avenues for states; the execution was haphazard. Today, anyone looking for order in the east-west progression of state names leading to Grand Boulevard won't find much.

As the street names were assigned, no thought was given to naming them after the original thirteen colonies, or the states of the Midwest, or putting them in alphabetical order. In order, they are, more or less, Mississippi, Wisconsin, Illinois, Missouri, and Indiana east of Jefferson. West of Jefferson are Texas, Ohio, Iowa, California, Oregon, Nebraska, Pennsylvania, Minnesota, Michigan, Virginia, Louisiana, Tennessee, and Arkansas Avenues. Altogether, the city has thirty-two streets with state names, twenty-nine of which are on the South Side. After St. Louis absorbed Carondelet in 1870, many of its north-south streets assumed the names of state streets that connected from St. Louis. In 1902, five additional streets to the south were named after the states of Alabama, Colorado, and Vermont and the territories of Alaska and Idaho.

Since there is no particular order among Indian names, the order in which they are placed isn't as confusing. Many of those names have been assigned to streets west of the original commons area. Cherokee, Chippewa, Meramec, Miami, and Dakota are among the streets named for tribes. Osceola Street is named for a Seminole Indian leader who fought against

Americans who tried to remove his people from their land in Florida. Potomac is named for the Potomac River. *Potomac* is an Indian word that John Smith recorded as *Potawameak*—"where goods are brought in"—in 1608.

Those names are sensible enough, but there are other east-west street names that seem like they should be Indian but are not. Itaska Street sounds like it should be Indian, but it's actually a misspelling of Lake Itasca, Minnesota. After he identified the lake as the source of the Mississippi River, Henry Rowe Schoolcraft formed the name from Latin words meaning "true source." And street names that seem to be for states actually are Indian names. The east-west Wyoming Place and Wyoming Street came from the Indian word for "land largely the big plain." The same goes for the east-west Utah Place and Utah Street, which is for the Ute or Utah Indians. Connecticut Street, which runs east to west in the Tower Grove South, Kingshighway Hills, and Tilles Park neighborhoods, adds to the confusion. It doesn't honor a state, rather an insurance company. The name of the Connecticut Insurance Company, the financier of the Tower Grove and Grand Avenue Addition of 1881, will always be remembered by those who drive along that thoroughfare.

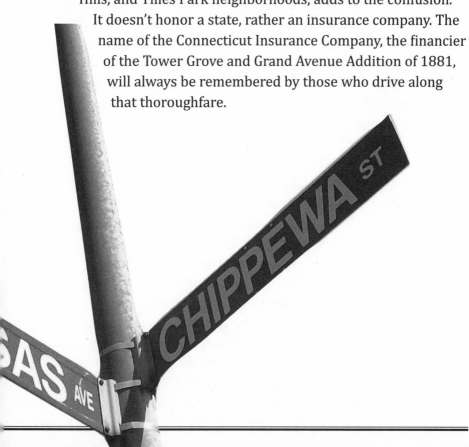

ALL IN A NAME

Immortality is one of the privileges of building a subdivision. William Federer, a developer of the Holly Hills neighborhood near Carondelet Park, used that privilege when he named a residential street Federer Place. Developer Gus Arendes will always be remembered by residents of Arendes Drive, while developer Donald Livingston is recalled by those on Livingston Drive. To ensure their wives also were remembered forever, the three Holly Hills developers created Marwinette Avenue. It's a composite of MARie Federer, WINifred Livingston, and JeanETTE Arendes.

The St. Louis Public Library's online street index, compiled by Dr. Glen Holt and Thomas A. Pearson, is filled with such attempts to immortalize people by putting their names on street signs. Kosciusko Street on the east end of Marine Villa and Soulard is named for Polish general Thaddeus Kosciusko, who fought for the patriots in the American Revolutionary War. He became a Polish hero when he fought for independence for Poland. Tamm Avenue commemorates Jacob Tamm, a farmer and landowner. On the South Side's far west end, Jamieson Avenue honors William and James Jamieson, two brothers who were early residents of that area. Morgan Ford Road was named for a road to a ford at the River des Peres operated by a man named Morgan. Carondelet landowner Edward Haren was supposed to have his own street, but a typo in the 1882 city ordinance rendered it Haven Street. The name stuck.

Street names aren't just for people. Sulphur Avenue was developed from a road leading to a sulphur spring in David W. Graham's Sulphur Spring tract. Hydraulic Avenue in Dutchtown was named for the nearby yard of the Hydraulic Press Brick Company. Hampton Avenue is named for an urban district in Middlesex County, England. Grand is the name for a truly grand 450-foot-wide boulevard proposed in 1850 by real estate developer Hiram W. Leffingwell. In the 1860s, the St. Louis County Court set the width at a more reasonable eighty feet. From the 1800s to the early 1900s, it was Grand Avenue. Since then the city has called it Grand Boulevard. The message hasn't gotten to many who still call it Grand Avenue. South Siders don't like change.

THE BROKEN ROAD

Residents of more than seven dozen South Side streets share the same broken tale. Ten minutes after company is due at their house on Itaska Street west of Francis Park, the host receives a desperate phone call. It's the guest, in a panic. He's at Itaska Street at Ridgewood Avenue. The street just ended. What should he do? The host gives him directions and mumbles how silly it is that somebody gave the same name to an east-west street on the east side of the South Side and an east-west street on the west side of the South Side.

The question has occurred to people who live on at least ninety South Side streets. In fact, they live on at least 250 separate streets with beginnings and ends. But because they more or less were parallel, people assigned the same names to those streets, oblivious to the grief it would cause to people trying to locate addresses in the future.

In a few cases, the streets were divided by Interstates 44 and 55. The meanderings of the Oak Hill Branch of the Union Pacific Railroad through the South Side were occasionally responsible for the confusion. Sometimes a park or another major obstacle caused the road to stop. Usually, the namers could choose different names, but instead they made the decision that would cause the most confusion. So it was that there are five separate streets with the name Clifton Avenue, five named Tholozan Avenue, and five named Missouri Avenue. There are seven different streets with the name Virginia Avenue.

If an enemy takes over and we decide to confuse our invaders with our streets, we don't have to do a thing. We'll be ready.

THE SOUTH SIDE ROLLING STOP

Former South Side alderwoman Jennifer Florida had a way of aggravating constituents. It's not that she wouldn't return phone calls or go against the wishes of residents on neighborhood issues. It's just a bad habit she picked up when she was growing up in central Illinois. When she came to a stop sign, she did what the sign says. "I come to an absolute stop. Sometimes people honk at me," said Florida, who was named St. Louis recorder of deeds in 2014. Around the South Side, it seems, most people don't have to worry about having an odd habit like Florida's. In a half-hour one Sunday afternoon, fifty westbound motorists on Fyler Avenue were spotted approaching a stop sign at Macklind Avenue. Only seven of them stopped, as in, their wheels stopped moving. Some of those apparently did so because traffic from Macklind stopped them from going forward. The others tapped their brakes with different degrees of firmness.

For what it's worth, the forty-three tappers committed a crime. The city traffic code really does require drivers to stop at a stop sign. For those who aren't sure of the meaning of "stop," the code offers a definition: "'Stop' means the complete cessation from movement." Anyone convicted of that crime must pay a fine of up to five hundred dollars and technically could spend up to ninety days in jail. Police would be ready to dispatch justice if they saw somebody committing such a crime, a police spokeswoman said. "If a motorist rolls or fails to stop, it is a violation of a city ordinance. If an officer sees this, the driver would in all likelihood be issued a ticket," spokeswoman Katie O'Sullivan said.

In the parking lot of the Shop 'n Save at 4660 Chippewa Street, people had various thoughts about the South Side stop. Will Phillips of Holly Hills acknowledged he doesn't always stop at stop signs. Whether the law should be enforced depends on the intersections, he said. Bill Wagner of the Southampton neighborhood would stop, but on one condition: "It depends whether there's a cop behind or not." Mike Pitts, a corrugated display designer living in Dutchtown, was alarmed when he learned how few people halt their vehicles at stop signs. "That's scary," he said. "I come to a complete stop. I aggravate a lot of people, but I do it anyway."

If just about everybody on the South Side goes through stop signs, there's good reason. There's about eighteen thousand stop signs in the city, compared with about six hundred traffic signals, street commissioner Todd Waelterman said. When people encounter three or four stop signs in ten blocks, it's easy to nudge the brake rather than press down hard, especially when the cops don't care. And yet people keep asking for more. "Certainly, I think we oftentimes misuse stop signs," Waelterman said. People try to use them to slow motorists down, Waelterman said. Neighbors keep pressuring for more signs. When people ask for a sign, the street department makes a study to see if it's needed. But regardless of what that recommendation might be, an alderman is still free to put forth a bill requiring another sign. "The neighborhood pressure is so great that it winds up becoming an ordinance and we wind up putting up a sign," Waelterman said.

Florida sees the pressure in her own ward. "People think that's the quick fix," she said. "You put up a stop sign, and people roll through it." She once sought to have police ticket all violators. "It's enforcement that really changes behavior in neighborhoods," she said. But the request didn't go anywhere. Instead, the stoppers keep on rolling, and rolling, and rolling.

THE STREET THAT ENDS WITH A STAIRWAY

On the South Side, some streets stop at circular concrete barriers set side by side. Some end at gates, some at Interstates 44 and 55, and some at railroad tracks. Others end at fences or at a river, but one street in the Gravois Park neighborhood halts in a completely different way: at a stairway. Motorists driving south on Oregon Avenue from Potomac Street toward Miami Street find that it suddenly stops at a stairway marked by a high wrought-iron fence. The fence is on the top of a concrete retaining wall that drops down eight feet. A car thief who is speeding away from police at 120 miles an hour might not want to choose southbound Oregon at Potomac for his escape path. Otherwise, if he was able to plow through the fence, he would find himself airborne in the best tradition of movie chase scenes.

The city's Board of Public Service apparently put up the wall at the behest of Oregon Avenue property owners who didn't like the way the street sloped. In the early 1920s, it filled with two- and four-family flats. In 1928, the Board of Aldermen passed an ordinance requiring property owners on the block to pay for a project to flatten out the street and make it end at a fence on top of an eight-foot retaining wall. Pedestrians could use the steps to walk from the lower part of Oregon to the upper part. More than eighty years after the project, Mike Seemiller of the Board of Public Service remarked that he'd never seen anything like this before. "This is a real unusual case," said Seemiller, whose agency is in charge of street construction.

The oddity benefits people like Sam Brown. He's a carpenter who lives in a four-family flat just north of the fence. "There's no through traffic. I like that part of it," Brown said. Pedestrians once could walk on a sidewalk to an opening in the fence and then go down a stairway, but that way through has been closed, to the consternation of some walkers. "I saw a man this morning walking. I saw him walk down to that fence and just look," said Jim Roos, who manages most of the four-family flats that line the street. It's not often that drivers or walkers come into the street and discover it stops, Roos said. By now, most people know that the street dead-ends, he said, but the way it dead-ends is like nowhere else.

Just before 9:30 on a Wednesday morning in June, an engine, four cars carrying freight, and a caboose crossed McRee Avenue east of Kingshighway Boulevard. Soon, a track took them under Interstate 44 as the train started a seven-mile winding trip through the South Side. The St. Louis, Oak Hill, and Carondelet Railway built the line in 1887. For more than 120 years, trains have made that trip, which snakes west, just west of Tower Grove Park, and southeast to the edge of Carondelet Park before heading south to the city line. Today, an average of four trains a day use the tracks, which are part of Union Pacific Railroad's DeSoto Subdivision from McRee Avenue to Poplar Bluff. People generally see the trains when they cross streets, but mostly the trains and the tracks they use are hidden by buildings, trees, brush, and by their location below street level. When they see the trains crossing a variety of different streets, motorists may think there's several lines on the South Side. But outside of the track that runs along the river, this is the only rail line south of Interstate 44 in the city.

After emerging from under Interstate 44 from McRee, the trains travel northwest of Vandeventer Avenue until they go underneath the Kingshighway Viaduct. They pass Bischoff Avenue before traveling under Southwest and Columbia Avenues on the east side of Marconi Avenue. Customers of Favazza's Restaurant on the Hill at Southwest and Marconi may not realize it, but their parking lot is just a few feet from train tracks. They can't see them because the tracks are below grade and because trees, brush, and a fence hide them, but if they come close to the trees and look through the brush, they will see the tracks, along with graffiti on the bridge on Southwest Avenue. More graffiti is evident to a person standing on the far side of the Columbia Avenue Bridge over the rail line. It covers a healthy portion of the side of a building owned by Ralston Purina at 5100 Columbia Avenue.

The train tracks continue below street level, between the industrial buildings on Hereford Street to the east and a mix of industries and old houses on Brannon Avenue to the west. Shoppers at the Schnucks on Arsenal Street may not know that train tracks are just

west of the parking lot unless they use the crosswalk of the bridge over the tracks. The tracks continue out of sight until they come in view on the trestle above Kingshighway just south of Home Depot. They're visible again from a bridge over the tracks on Morgan Ford Road near Fairview Avenue. The tracks continue on bridges over Chippewa Street and Gravois Avenue before mostly staying behind industrial buildings around Gustine, Ulena, and Dewey Avenues. Things may look inviting a hundred feet away, on the other side of the trees and overgrowth, but there is plenty of dirt, trash, and graffiti along the rail line.

From the north, the rail line goes under the bridge leading from Grand Boulevard into Carondelet Park. It passes under another bridge leading from the west part of the park to the Carondelet Park Recplex. Those who drop off their papers or aluminum cans in the park's recycling center can see a long open section of the tracks. South of the spot, the tracks go under Loughborough Avenue and by the Loughborough Commons Shopping Center. From there, they go under Interstate 55, between Alabama and Alaska Avenues and out of the city. Their route is on city maps, but most people don't notice. Though the rails are in the South Side, for most they're in another world.

SOUTH SIDE NATIONAL BANK

Unlike many major street corners, there is no Walgreens at Gravois Avenue and Grand Boulevard. That's good, because if there was one a key link to the area's past would be gone. In the late 1990s, neighborhood groups stopped the demolition of the South Side National Bank at the southwest corner of Grand and Gravois and its replacement by a smaller bank building and a Walgreens. The grand ten-story Art Deco building the preservationists saved was seen as a sign the good times would go on forever when it opened just before the start of the Depression. A booklet put out when it opened on January 2, 1929, called it "The Dawn of a New Day for Grand and Gravois."

Like so much on the South Side, Anheuser-Busch had a hand in the bank. Beer baron Adolphus Busch founded the South Side Bank at the beginning of the 1890s. The Busches stayed involved in the bank at Broadway and Pestalozzi Street and its successor, the South Side Trust Co. Busches were on the bank board in 1927 when it voted to buy land on the southwest corner of Grand and Gravois for a new building. The next year, the bank merged with Farmers and Merchants Trust, which was on the southeast corner of Grand and Gravois.

With the strength of two banks, the owners had reason for optimism when they opened the new building in 1929. "The Dawn of a New Day" spoke of how the bank was on the second floor, accessible by a grand staircase and an elevator "to give you and the other citizens of South St. Louis first-class protection." Apparently, they thought that would discourage bank robbers. But protection from bandits didn't protect the bank from closing and reorganizing during the Depression. Nonetheless, a bank stayed at the corner through changes in the area and the attempt to tear it down.

In 2001, after neighborhood groups saved the building, Allegiant Bancorp Inc. gave the building to the Grand Oak Hill Community Corp., a neighborhood group. Grand Oak Hill later gave it to the Lawrence Group, a local architectural firm. The Lawrence Group rehabbed the building for thirteen condominiums on seven top floors and improved three bottom floors for commercial use, but the economic downturn slowed efforts to occupy the whole building.

Residents of the building—now called the South Side Tower—can ease their worries about that downturn or anything else by going to its rooftop. There, they have a hawk's-eye view of the South Side, downtown, and the building Walgreens put up when it couldn't tear down the South Side National Bank.

In a shady spot in Tower Grove Park on a Sunday afternoon, a mother places a tablecloth on a picnic table. In a language other than English, she calls her husband and children to sit down. Lunch is about to begin. Members of other families walking on paths nearby are also talking in a language other than English, but not the language of the family preparing for a picnic lunch. It's a story that could have been told about the park in 1900 or 2010. In the earlier period, the non-English languages of park users could have been German, Polish, or Italian. Today, it might be Vietnamese, Bosnian, or Spanish.

The story told by Tower Grove Park director John Karel is one example of what he sees as an enormous consistency in what has gone on at the park for more than 140 years. The vision Missouri Botanical Garden founder Henry Shaw had when he gave St. Louis land for the park in 1868 is to a large degree a reality today. Cars long ago replaced horse buggies as the way to traverse the park, but the park that visitors see today is much the same as the one Mark Twain

Green House, Tower Grove Park, St. Lo

praised following a visit during an 1882 tour of towns and cities along the Mississippi River. In *Life on the Mississippi*, Twain wrote that Tower Grove Park, Forest Park, and the Missouri Botanical Garden were notable among the fine parks of St. Louis. The map he would have used to travel the park is the same as visitors now use.

Many of the structures Twain saw in 1882 still serve the same purpose. Stable buildings are still stable buildings. Mock ruins assembled from what was left after a fire destroyed the first Lindell Hotel in 1867 are still there. So are the water lilies. Statues Shaw donated of Shakespeare, Mozart, and others are as he left them. Music is still heard weekly in the summer, but at a different time. In the nineteenth century, it was from 4 P.M. to

6 P.M. on Sundays, when people of all classes could come. Today, the Compton Heights Concert Band plays at 7:30 P.M. on Mondays. And if Twain were to return today, he would find the four stone main entrances the same as the last time he was here.

Karel acknowledges there are differences between the park today and the one of the late nineteenth century. Nonetheless, the similarities are strong enough to make Tower Grove almost unprecedented among American parks, Karel contends. As before, thousands of trees cover the 289-acre park surrounded by Grand Boulevard, Arsenal Street, Kingshighway Boulevard, and Magnolia Avenue. Karel speculates that about 120 of the park's trees are original. Many other trees among the 6,500 or so are also old but probably were planted after Shaw died in 1889, Karel said. And there are new uses, including the farmers' market that now operates in the park in the spring, summer, and fall.

Though the park long was a treasure, many worried that it would be lost. That's what people thought when Karel became director in 1987. "It didn't seem to be a sure thing that we were going to survive," said Karel, who directed Missouri's state park system from 1979 to 1985. But along with other South Siders, he was determined to stop the decline. "We weren't going to go down without a fight," Karel said, but there were reasons for discouragement. The Piper Palm House, built to house palms in 1878, was used as a garage. The roof was leaking, and mortar was crumbling from between rows of bricks, but after restoration, the building became an elegant place for Sunday brunches and receptions. Its acoustics make it a favorite place to hear members of the St. Louis Symphony Orchestra perform works by Beethoven and Mozart. The success of the Piper Palm House was contagious throughout the park. Henry Shaw established a board to govern the park, while the city was charged to maintain the land. But private donors raised the millions of dollars necessary to complete the restoration. Today, the park is a place of wonder for those who come for a visit, be they from across the street, West County, or China. Whatever they say, and whatever the visitors' language, their words would please Shaw if he were to hear them today.

A DOME SAVED A GARDEN

From 1960 on, people were excited about Shaw's Garden in a way they hadn't been in years. Shaw's Garden was what people half a century ago called the Missouri Botanical Garden. Whatever people called it, the buzz was about a new attraction that opened late in 1960 to replace the outdated Palm House: the Climatron. A geodesic dome modeled after the designs of R. Buckminster Fuller, the upside-down plexiglass-enclosed bowl showed all that was possible in a greenhouse. It was 70 feet high, 175 feet in diameter, and covered three-quarters of an acre. In a tropical environment, it contained banana plants, coffee plants, palms, and a whole array of other tropical and semi-tropical plants owned by the garden.

After it opened in October 1960, the papers gushed about this building that offered different climates, depending where a person was in the dome. "The gleaming transparent dome of

aluminum and plexiglass is the climax of a long chain of engineering triumphs, some laboriously arrived at and inconceiv-
able without the aid of electronic computers, others the result
of brilliant improvisations," the *Post-Dispatch* said in an article
titled "The Climatron as Architecture." In an article written in
the coldest days of January 1961, the *Globe-Democrat* spoke
of the St. Louisan imagining he was in a warmer place. "In his
dreams of escape to Caribbean islands or remote spots south
in the sun, he may overlook a place considerably closer—the
Climatron in Missouri Botanical (Shaw's) Garden."

The superlatives attached to the Climatron were great, but
the biggest one was how it turned around a slide in attendance
at the garden that started with the Depression. So few people
paid to get in that the garden couldn't afford to change exhibits.
Buildings were in poor shape. The future looked grim. But then
came the Climatron, along with thousands of people willing to
pay the fifty-cent admission fee at the new attraction. Attendance, which had been as low as 156,297 in 1955, climbed from
279,800 in 1959 to 423,302 in 1960. It kept increasing from
there. Today, more than 970,000 people come to the garden
each year. It's possible Shaw's Garden wouldn't have developed
into the marvel for visitors and researchers that it is today if
the Climatron hadn't been built.

The intent was innocent enough: put up money to find somebody to make a monument to the way three journalists showed the German-American spirit in St. Louis. So why were people yelling? Well, the monument was of a woman, and she wasn't wearing clothes, and this was 1913. So it was that 250 people sent letters condemning the design of German sculptor Wilhelm Wandschneider for a memorial to honor journalists Carl Schurz, Emil Preetorius, and Carl Daenzer. Wandschneider was on his way from Germany to accept the commission, and the committee that chose the design was looking for a way out.

All three of the journalists had been editors of the *Westliche Post*, the local German-language newspaper. Schurz had been a Civil War general, a senator from Missouri, and secretary of the interior under President Rutherford Hayes. A group formed to honor them, and Adolphus Busch of Anheuser-Busch put up $20,000 for a memorial—nearly $430,000 in 2014 dollars. Others added more. The competition began. When it was over, a committee accepted Wandschneider's design of a seated nude woman holding torches in each of her outstretched arms. He called it *The Naked Truth*.

Then the protests began. Busch said the design was too startling to accept. The $30,000 contract and $1,000 bonus were withdrawn. It was too much for Dr. Frederick Kolben-heyer, who had headed a committee that selected Wand-schneider's design out of seven considered. "Gentlemen," he said to the directors of the Schurz-Preetorius-Daenzer Memorial Association, "you are a lot of damned fools. I resign." The nude woman's figure typified the naked truth the three great German-American editors fought for, he said. "The torches which the figure holds in each hand are for the enlightening of Germany and America." An editorial in the

St. Louis Post-Dispatch said *The Naked Truth* was a frequent troublemaker.

Meanwhile, Wandschneider sailed for the United States with his wife to accept his prize. When he arrived in New York, he threatened to sue or set off an international incident if he didn't get it. He refused an offer to compromise by draping the lady with lingerie. When he showed up in St. Louis on May 29, the statue was big news. The committee that made the selection wasn't sure what to do. After a hot May, some said Wandschneider had clad the woman for St. Louis summers. The *St. Louis Globe-Democrat* remarked that *The Naked Truth* may be a fine monument for some newspapers, but reputable newspapers don't print every truth they hear, the paper said, because they learned it in confidence or it may hurt innocent people.

Then Busch announced he'd taken a good look at a model of the statue. It was fine, he said, adding that he'd drawn his first conclusions after looking at sketches. That was enough for the board of the association that commissioned the monument. It voted 12–2 in favor of Wandschneider's design. The statue was dedicated for all to see on May 27, 1914, in Compton Hill Reservoir Park on South Grand Boulevard near the present site of Interstate 44.

Other pitfalls were ahead for the statue. After the United States entered World War I, some suggested the statue be melted down for cannonballs meant for Germans. Fortunately, the idea remained only a suggestion. In the 1960s, it was moved out of the path of the new Interstate 44. In recent years it started looking seedy. Graffiti artists dabbed paint on her toenails, fingernails, and lips. It fell to neighborhood groups to raise money to restore the lady.

Today, the statue sits peacefully in Compton Hill Reservoir Park as a monument to a time when naked truth was an embarrassment.

Even partially covered by various shades of blue and purple paint, the Frog of Chippewa Street carries a kind of dignity. Crouched in the middle of what was once a vacant lot at Chippewa Street and Oregon Avenue, the frog stands four feet high and is five and a half feet long and four feet wide. The statue had no ordinary beginning. It is one of about forty concrete cast frogs made by Bob Cassilly, who created Turtle Park near Forest Park and founded the City Museum downtown. Once people bought the frogs, they wound up in all kinds of places. One of those places was a quarter-acre vacant lot that was once the location of a 7-Eleven convenience store. Mark Rice, who lives a few blocks away, got a grant to buy the frog and place it on the lot. It was meant to be a sign that the area was hopping back. But at times things seemed more like the place was croaking.

Before the frog came, the appearance of the place wasn't particularly inviting. The 7-Eleven was torn down, but the empty lot was filled with junk cars and broken glass. The frog brought hope and plenty of promises from people to help Rice keep it up. Nobody followed through. Rice maintained the property for a while before he gave up. Almus "Slim" Cox, a business and community leader and the longtime owner of Slim and Zella Mae Cox Furniture next to the lot, said he and his wife had tried to maintain the park, but they grew too old and couldn't continue.

THE FROG -of- CHIPPEWA ST.

So it was that for some years people cut the grass regularly and kept up the plants. In other years, it became overgrown until nobody could see the frog. Paint once applied by a group of volunteers started chipping off, leaving strange splotches. More recently, the Chippewa-Broadway Business Association offered a hand to bring out the best in what became known as the Frog Garden.

With their help, groups such as workers from a nearby branch of Regions Bank and the group Faith Beyond Walls installed planter boxes, put in mulch and wood chips, and planted flowers, including daffodil bulbs donated by the Missouri Botanical Garden. The work of the volunteers is made more difficult by the fact that nobody really owns the park. The land is registered to something called the Chippewa-Broadway Jefferson Association, but that group no longer exists. Only time will tell how long the work of the volunteers at the Frog Park will continue. But whatever happens in the future, nothing can take away the dignity of the Frog of Chippewa Street.

On a parking lot on Chippewa Street a plastic spoon rested amidst a runny brownish-white glob. A minute before, it was a medium Ted Drewes hot fudge concrete with a spoon in the middle, but then the holder of that treasured treat turned it over to test the claim that if you held a concrete upside-down, it would stay in place, along with the spoon. It stayed in the cup for only a moment before plopping to the ground. Crestfallen, but still craving what only Ted Drewes can offer, the man who turned the concrete over eventually made his way back to a window and bought another one.

The failed experiment took place early on a dreary Saturday evening in May amidst a more modest crowd compared with the hot August weekend evening throngs that spill out onto Chippewa, but the group of customers still was big enough that the windows had constant lines. Among those who had come was a woman with bright pink hair, a wedding party, a couple and their four children on vacation from Minnesota, and people who had returned from afar to taste this South Side delight.

Walt and Kim Wiseman stop by every time they make the eighty-mile trip to St. Louis. Kim's grandmother lives near the Bevo Mill, so they come in about once a month. "Best place to eat ice cream," said Walt, a carpenter, eating his Dutchman. Kim usually buys the Dutchman, but this time she tried something new, the Christy. Their son Danny feasted on a large Dutchman concrete. Pete and Pat Lecko and their twenty-year-old son David only had to travel from south St. Louis County to come to Ted Drewes. They come about twice a month. Pat grew up not far from the Ted Drewes at 4224 South Grand Boulevard and always went there. "I think it's great ice cream," Pat said. "I've been to other custard places. I don't like them as much as here." David, who attends Missouri University of Science and Technology at Rolla, pledges his eternal devotion. "I'll be coming here my entire life. The ice cream's so good."

It's pretty well known around St. Louis how the Ted Drewes stores came about. In 1929, Ted Sr. opened his first store in Florida. He opened another one on Natural Bridge Road in 1930 and then the

South Grand outlet in 1931. Ten years later, the Chippewa store opened. The Natural Bridge location closed in the late 1950s, leaving just the two on the South Side. Ted Jr., who's now in charge, has often said he's turned down numerous offers to franchise his operation because it could lead to a mediocre product. Instead, he has worked on building up a loyalty that crosses generations. People love this place and what comes out of it, even if the concretes don't always stay in the cup. The loyalty extends so far that a trip to Ted's is another ritual of life in St. Louis, for residents and visitors alike. Patrons believe the Ted Drewes slogan, "It really is good, guys, and gals."

It's terrific, but it's still just fancy ice cream. Other places sell frozen treats that might beat a Ted Drewes concrete in a blind taste test, but people don't stand in line in August when the mercury's passed one hundred to buy one of those other items. Hungry customers don't routinely stop at other establishments before the prom or after a meal at Charlie Gitto's on the Hill. Something else happened to elevate Ted Drewes to the short list of must-see places for tourists to go when they're in St. Louis. Things came together. It helped that the main store is on historic Route 66, close to everything. It's wholesome and clean, which makes it a great place to bring the kids and for teenagers to hang out. When those kids and teenagers grow up, they'll bring their kids and teenagers to Ted Drewes. Then there's the ritual people go through to buy and consume something at Ted Drewes. Get into a line spilling out onto Chippewa, wait, order, pay, take the treat, stand around with others, and roll that cold goodness around in your mouth. It's an odd ritual, but pleasant, the kind of experience that makes for tradition. Let people all over St. Louis experience it, along with tourists and former St. Louisans back for a visit, and the tradition becomes an institution.

SAVING THE FEASTING FOX

Martin and Susan Luepker owned a healthy heating and air conditioning business that Martin's grandfather started in 1896. The couple knew nothing about the restaurant business. So why would they want to acquire a broken-down old building, renovate it, and run a European-style restaurant there? All good questions. The answer boils down to the fact that they didn't want the Dutchtown neighborhood to lose a historic building that was part of the effort of Anheuser-Busch to stave off Prohibition. Today, their Al Smith's Feasting Fox Restaurant is a popular place full of antiques and brewery collectibles known for its American and German dishes.

In 1914, August Busch Sr. opened the Gretchen Inn at South Grand Boulevard and Meramec Street. It was the second of three nearby restaurants that the Busches opened in the same decade. The Stork Inn at Virginia and Taft Avenues was built in 1910, and the Bevo Mill at Morgan Ford Road and Gravois Avenue in 1917. The Gretchen Inn was a popular place along busy Grand Boulevard, in part because of a racetrack on the southwest corner of Meramec and Grand called Priester's Park.

The coming of Prohibition in 1920 brought more changes to the building than the removal of alcohol from the menu. It became a store where legal products made by Budweiser, such as vitamins, ice cream, soda, and spices, were sold. After the repeal of Prohibition in 1933, antitrust laws wouldn't allow a brewery to operate a place where drinks were sold. So the brewery leased it to Al Smith, who operated it until 1961. Then Fred and Evelyn Krumm, who had managed the restaurant since 1945, took over. After it closed in 1986, the building started falling apart. In 1993, Anheuser-Busch took steps to sell it to a fast-food restaurant.

Neighbors wouldn't have it and started noisy and well-publicized protests. The brewery backed down and said it would entertain other proposals. Then the Luepkers reluctantly entered the picture and agreed to take on the project. "We thought more or less if we didn't do it there's nobody else who would," Martin said. So the couple plowed ahead to renovate a building that was structurally solid but otherwise a mess. The windows were boarded up, parts of the roof were missing, and the ceiling had collapsed over the kitchen. All of the original woodwork was gone. As they did their renovations, they looked for furniture from other old restaurants: Top of the 230 in Clayton, the Missouri Athletic Club, the old Dohack's Restaurant on Lemay Ferry Road, and Nantucket Cove. "The building wanted to live. Whatever we needed came," Martin said. Publicity over the opening in 1994 brought more business than the Luepkers could handle. In 1997, the couple opened the Gretchen Inn for banquets in an adjacent building. It's been a major part of the business. Today, the restaurant is filled with a wide mix of memorabilia. One framed 1896 picture shows a print of Union Station by the Anheuser-Busch Brewing Association. Another shows Custer's Last Stand. One old sign reads, "Best Since 1867 Leinenkugels Chippewa's Pride."

Customers seem pleased with the restaurant's fare. "I love the Feasting Fox. I love coming in here because of the eclectic atmosphere," said Vicki Gallant, who has lived in the neighborhood for ten years. "We've been coming here for years, and we know Martin and Sue, the owners," said Shannon Olson, a Florissant resident who was eating lunch with her family. The next step is uncertain for the Luepkers. "Sooner or later, we're going to be too old. We haven't anyone in our family that's interested," Martin said. But Susan has confidence in its future. "Just like in the beginning, the building wanted to be saved and it will be again," she said.

The oft-told tale on the South Side is that Anheuser-Busch president August Busch Sr. built the Bevo Mill at Morgan Ford Road and Gravois Avenue as a place to rest halfway between the Anheuser-Busch brewery and Grant's Farm, but the big reason was to fight the Prohibitionist idea that alcohol was evil and that places serving alcohol were not for polite people. Busch wanted to show that people could enjoy light wine, a beer, or near beer with good food and the atmosphere of a German family garden.

In June 1917, the restaurant opened in a $200,000 structure with a tower supporting a Dutch windmill. It seated seven hundred inside and out. Busch wanted to give the place an Old World feel. And one way was with a new near beer called Bevo. Bevo, beer, and light wine were the only adult beverages available.

The Bevo Mill became a popular attraction, but it wasn't without its detractors. In their book, *Under the Influence: The Unauthorized Story of the Anheuser-Busch Dynasty*, Peter Hernon and Terry Ganey wrote that in spite of what Busch said, patrons of German saloons preferred hard liquor over the less intoxicating variety. "More serious, the idea ran afoul of wartime hysteria," they wrote. "There were cries that the mill, with its slowly revolving blades and Teutonic menu featuring such heavy delicacies as bratwurst glockein, was an insidious attempt to force German ways upon patriotic St. Louis."

But the Bevo Mill survived those attacks as it survived Prohibition. It stayed on as a South Side landmark and a favorite place to order sauerbraten. It gave its name to the surrounding neighborhood. In 2009, it survived the sudden closing of its doors that caused many to lose deposits they had placed on wedding receptions. Today, under new owners, it is again a destination for Sunday brunch and a place for wedding receptions. It remains one of the brewery's biggest gifts to the South Side.

THE CASA LOMA

If a big band was big, it made it to the Casa Loma Ballroom. Glenn Miller came there. So did Tommy Dorsey, Guy Lombardo, Duke Ellington, Louis Armstrong, and Frank Sinatra. Bill Haley and the Comets rocked around the clock at the ballroom at 3354 Iowa Avenue. For decades, men in suits and women in fancy dresses packed the dance floor of the place around the corner from the Cherokee Street shopping district. Today, they're still coming. Pat Brannon, who owns the ballroom, brings in eighteen- to twenty-four-piece big band orchestras on Fridays, old-time rock 'n' roll or swing on Saturdays, and Hispanic dances with out-of-town bands on Sundays.

Brannon was sales manager for a fence company when he bought the ballroom in 1990. "I just happened to come in and saw it was for sale," Brannon said. "I'd been an Imperial swing dancer for years and had always been on the outside of the bar and figured it wouldn't be that hard to be on the inside of the bar," he said. "They haven't kicked me out yet." Crowds vary. "You can have three hundred on a Saturday night, or you can have six hundred," Brannon said. He maintains diverse acts. For lovers of the big bands, he's had Larry O'Brien and the Glenn Miller Orchestra and Guy Lombardo's Royal Canadians with Al Pierson. For those who crave a different sound, he's had Sh-Boom, Butch Wax and the Hollywoods, and the Smash Band.

The ballroom itself looks pretty much like pictures of the original Casa Loma. Balcony seating is available on three sides, and the raised stage is on the fourth. On either side of the stage, banners advertising Corona Extra hang down. On one side of the stage is a black-and-white drawing of a 1930s-era man in a tux with a woman in formal dress. Black tables and chairs surround the hardwood dance floor. Near the entrance, a bulletin board displays pictures of such stars and groups as Bob Kuban, Gateway City Big Band, and Hudson and the Hoo Doo Cats. A stairway leads to the entrance.

On the Saturday afternoon of Memorial Day weekend in 2010, a different kind of entertainment was planned. Steve Vollenweider, a college student studying architecture, was preparing for a benefit for the American Diabetes Association that night. The Hill resident organized live music tributes to Nina Simone, Johnny Cash, Elvis Presley, and Michael Jackson. He rented the place hoping to bring in lots of cash for his cause. He had reason for choosing the Casa Loma. "Casa Loma is very historic, and it's something that I believe we should support in this city," he said.

The venue's history began when a building with a ballroom was put up on that site in 1927. In his book *St. Louis Casa Loma Ballroom*, David A. Lossos noted there were five different attempts to open a ballroom there, beginning with one called Cinderella Hall. All failed. Art Kawall and H. J. "Nap" Burian tried again in 1935. They took the name Casa Loma from the popular Glen Gray's Casa Loma Band. Success followed, and the Casa Loma brought in groups that included the

Count Basie Orchestra and Skitch Henderson, who later played on *The Tonight Show*. It seemed that nothing could go wrong, but something did. On the bitterly cold evening of January 19, 1940, a fire destroyed the building. Marvin "Bud" Miller was sixteen when he witnessed the fire. He recalled his impressions in a March 27, 1994, article about the blaze in the *South Side Journal*. "It was amazing to watch. Of course, this was a landmark place . . . to see all of this destruction, and to see all these men performing in that bitter cold, it was just incredible." The work of the firefighters that night was one of the reasons he made firefighting a career.

The damage was total, but the hunger for the big band sound was great. On November 15, 1940, Herbie Kay and His Orchestra performed on opening night of the rebuilt Casa Loma. In the war years that followed, the area needed the good times the dance hall provided. At its height, as many as three thousand came out. The place was open six nights a week. But times changed. Burian died in 1958. By the 1960s, the Casa Loma was open three nights a week. The Kawall family sold it in 1967. Music was offered both for a younger and an older crowd. Although attendance was down to four or five hundred a night, it was still profitable. It kept being profitable. Some would say that a place started for the musical tastes of the 1930s wouldn't be around in the twenty-first century, but ballroom music remains popular, which keeps the Casa Loma humming.

THE PELICAN'S SAD END

For years, people remembered the restaurant at 2256 South Grand Boulevard for the twenty-five-foot blue pelican sign. The establishment had a variety of owners and names, but its longest tenure went by the name Pelican's, named after its owner James Pelican, who began operations in the 1930s.

As early as 1875, people were eating and drinking at that location. Three years later, one C. Becker was given a building permit to build an addition to the "existing saloon and dwelling." A 1979 *Globe-Democrat* story said that the Griesedieck family of brewers, which later bought Falstaff Brewing Company, was the owner during this period. In 1895, the family spent four thousand dollars to build an addition, including the turret on the corner that gave the building its present look. Before Prohibition, the eatery was known as the Anschuetz Restaurant. A 1969 *Post-Dispatch* article on the restaurant offered this observation by writer Ron Powers about then-owner Nick Laskaris: "Legends that cast Pelican's as a one-time speakeasy abound, but Laskaris denies knowledge of any such thing, deadpan." It is known more definitely what happened in the back of the restaurant during the 1920s. The Lami Real Estate Company rented that area to the Famous Players Corporation for an open-air movie theater.

In 1938, Pelican became the owner and hired the chef who would develop the restaurant's distinctive menu. Thomas Pisani, who later became part owner, prepared specialties including fillet of sole, potato pancakes, sauerbraten, stuffed deviled crabs, and stewed chicken and dumplings. Turtle soup, however, stood at the top of the list. The soup—filled with vegetables, spices, and wine—remained a favorite of the restaurant's patrons after Laskaris leased it in 1956. "A cup of turtle soup, prepared in the Pelican's kitchen in a two-day process and emerging thick, dark and succulent, is a good starter," Powers wrote in the 1969 *Post-Dispatch* article about the restaurant. The creator of the soup, Pisani, retired because of poor health in 1974. What went into his soup became an issue after Laskaris gave up his lease in 1975 to devote all his time to the operation of Nico's Restaurant at 5046 Shaw Avenue. He took with him cooks Pisani had trained to prepare the favorite dish. Pisani's widow, Ruby, decided to keep the recipe to herself. "As far as I'm concerned, I'm going to hold onto that secret."

The restaurant opened under new management, Gabriel Shabbaugh. Although Pisani's widow refused to disclose the recipe, Shabbaugh claimed he learned it from a chef Pisani had taught. But the soup itself wasn't enough to keep the place open, and it closed in 1978. The next year, Mayor James Conway cut the ribbon for a new owner, Salim Hanna, who also claimed that a former chef had given him the original recipe. "The one used in the 1950s and 1960s was good," Hanna said. "But I promise you, ours will be better." But, again, it wasn't good enough to keep the place open. Hanna had served authentic Middle Eastern food with the soup before closing in 1982.

Shortly after Hanna shut the place down, a team made up of Charles Dreeba, James Ginther, A. J. Squiteri, and Robert M. Conway pitched in to reopen the place as Paddington and Worthmore's Pelican Café. It featured a menu that included sweet and sour meatballs, steamed shrimp, Kansas City steak, and prime rib. Old articles about the opening don't mention turtle soup. The partners seemed confident enough in their venture that they opened a second location in the old Slay's restaurant at 10203 Gravois Avenue in Affton in 1984. Conway, a redeveloper and former president of Tower Grove Bank and Trust Company, was often seen at both restaurants. Friends described him as friendly and effervescent, but he was hiding a darker side. Family members later told police Conway had been depressed about his business developments. That was how they reacted to the news that Conway set the restaurant on Grand on fire with charcoal briquettes and a flammable liquid early on the morning of June 16, 1985. Then he put a .38-caliber handgun to his head and pulled the trigger. He died late that night. The pelican sign fell into the hands of the city. Today, the sign is owned by the Antique Warehouse, a private museum, which specializes in signs and is located just beyond the boundaries of this book's subject. Different owners have restored the building for offices, but nobody has put a restaurant in it since.

FROM THE BRINK

When Ruth Kamphoefner bought a dilapidated Victorian mansion in Lafayette Square in 1970, she noticed some nice ladies walking around the neighborhood. At least they seemed nice to her. In fact, they were prostitutes. Nothing worked in the house, so she had basic plumbing and electrical work done, and replaced broken windows. Then came the rats and roaches. "We worked very fast. We found out the secrets of getting rid of roaches and getting rid of rats," Kamphoefner said. But it was harder to get rid of the rats and roaches who tore down historic houses and wanted to clear the neighborhood to make way for housing projects and a road called the North-South Distributor Highway. But Lafayette Square pioneers like Kamphoefner prevailed, and the neighborhood went on to be one of the prettiest in the South Side.

Kamphoefner told her family's story in *Lafayette Comes Back*, which she self-published in 2000. That story began when her husband suddenly died in 1964, leaving her family living on Social Security checks and her part-time job as an art teacher. Then one day in 1970, she learned a house was available in Lafayette Square for $15,000. It was a much better price than the $35,000 cost of a new three-bedroom house in Affton. So she went looking and found even better bargains. She chose a house at 1526 Mississippi Avenue that was selling for $2,700. "It was pretty bad," said Kamphoefner's daughter, Carol Surgant, who was fourteen when her mother bought the house. "We came into it very naive about everything." Roaches were especially bad before the family moved in, and they didn't respond to bug spray. Boric acid was more effective. So was a product in a tube called electric paste, but it smelled horrible, Surgant said. "We didn't move down there until we had gotten rid of all the roaches," she said.

When three of the eight rooms were ready, the family moved in and kept fixing up the house. But "ready" for the

Kamphoefners didn't mean ready for anybody else. Among other things, there wasn't a kitchen. "For the first year, we cooked on an electric hot plate," Surgant said. "It kind of was like camping out inside a house," she said. Meanwhile, as the five children explored their neighborhood, they found things they wouldn't find in a nicer area. Surgant and a brother found a drunk sleeping in weeds in an empty lot. Men came into the neighborhood looking for prostitutes.

Meanwhile, Kamphoefner worked with others in the community to save the neighborhood. It was lonely work. The main group working to save the neighborhood, the Lafayette Square Restoration Committee, had just enough people to sit around a table, but there were experts, including three engineers and a museum curator. There were enough people to start planting tulips in Lafayette Park. There were enough to fight against the forces that would destroy the neighborhood. In 1972, the Board of Aldermen approved a historic district designation for the neighborhood, which provided protection against demolition of historic buildings and required them to be held to historic standards. The neighbors received more good news in the form of a twenty-five thousand dollar loan from the National Trust for Historic Preservation to buy historic homes in danger of demolition. The naming of houses in Lafayette Square to the National Register of Historic Places made it more unlikely that a highway would be built through the neighborhood.

With all of this, and the addition of more pioneers, people started seeing major changes, and Kamphoefner kept working for the neighborhood. She sold her first home in 1983 and kept buying. Altogether, she bought eighteen homes in danger of demolition and resold them without a profit. She completely restored seven properties. She lived in a home on Preston Place until 2007, when she moved to a senior citizens apartment in Shrewsbury. Kamphoefner said, in 2010, she never became discouraged. "I think we were optimists all the time," she said. "I would do it again. If I were physically able to, I would do it again." Surgant has similar thoughts. "It was great. I'm glad I did that as a kid rather than living in suburbia."

THE WAYWARD STEEPLE

The near South Side's skyline is littered with an army of steeples. One steeple in particular has risen above the rest. For more than one hundred years, people have known there was something grand about St. Francis de Sales Catholic Church. With a three-hundred-foot steeple, the church at 2653 Ohio Avenue is a landmark on Gravois Avenue. After it was dedicated in 1908, it was a fitting replacement for a church demolished by the Great Cyclone of 1896. It was well beyond anything seven German immigrant dairymen could have imagined in 1867 when they bought a tract at Gravois and Ohio for a new parish that would become St. Francis de Sales. Designed to match a Gothic church in Germany, the building contains a 50-foot-tall high altar and a 130-foot-long aisle. The church interior is filled with Gothic arches and stained glass windows. It looked magnificent when seven to nine thousand families were part of a largely German-American parish. It kept that magnificence when attendance at Sunday Mass dropped to fifty or sixty, forcing the parish to close in 2005.

The parish doors being closed were only part of the church's problems. The building held a secret. A four-foot-deep concrete foundation, in poor condition, rests on soil beneath the much-admired steeple. The builders may have thought the foundation was sufficient, but in time, ever so slightly, the steeple started to move. No, the spire isn't in danger of crashing onto Gravois. The slow twist has shifted the spire only a fraction of an inch to the southeast, but it was enough to send cracks throughout the rest of the building. In the choir lofts, cracks developed that were at least a half-inch wide. Temporary repairs ensured that water can't get into the building. A stained glass window near the crack was removed in December 2009 after it bowed several inches toward the inside of the choir loft. Temporary repairs of the cracks kept water and the elements out. Permanent repairs, however, must wait until someone fixes the foundation. Without that fix, the church's long-term structural integrity is in danger, and when the parish closed, it seemed that no group or individual would be able to spearhead those repairs.

Then, at the same time the parish closed, St. Louis archbishop Raymond Burke did something that brought a new congregation to St. Francis de Sales and new hope for the steeple. He made a request to the Institute of Christ the King Sovereign Priest, a church body dedicated to the traditional Latin Mass. He asked the group to establish St. Francis de Sales as a place to celebrate that Mass. Instead of a parish, set up on geographical lines, it would be an oratory, where anyone could come. Today, there are two Masses each Sunday, drawing a combined total of about a thousand faithful. "Some people come only once a month. They drive up to three hours," said Canon Michael K. Wiener, rector at St. Francis de Sales. Repairs have been done on much of the oratory's campus, which includes two school buildings, a gym, a convent, a rectory, a vacant building, and the church. A charter school, the Knowledge Is

Power Program (KIPP) Inspire Academy operates on the church campus. The convent is being restored, and another building is being used by homeschoolers, a day care, and several choirs.

Now the St. Francis de Sales Oratory is looking ahead to the major task of repairing the steeple. An engineering firm determined in 2005 that a rock formation on which to lay a foundation was twenty feet below the ground. A problem was getting underneath to attach the new foundation to the old one. The oratory hopes to raise the money for the steeple tower before it turns to future work to preserve the exterior and interior. However, the congregation is young and not big enough to provide the money, Wiener said, but he has faith it will happen.

SPORTS ON A SUNDAY MORNING

A chance discussion over beer at a South Side bar on Labor Day 1944 affected more than ten thousand boys and girls who played youth sports for the next half-century. Oddly, those who were at Becker's Tavern weren't thinking about youth sports at all. They were talking about the soccer and baseball games a group of men had played since the 1920s in the Sunday Morning League at Carondelet Park. Then one of them, Earl Kessler, asked, "Why don't we enter a team in the Muny League?" That discussion led to the formation of the new Carondelet Sunday Morning Athletic Club (CSMAC) to put a team in the citywide Muny League. At first, the group provided a place for men to play baseball and soccer. It bought a building at 1012 Loughborough Avenue in 1946. Different buildings at that address would be at the center of the organization's work for the next sixty years, but then CSMAC branched out, and its efforts truly became memorable. CSMAC is most remembered for its work with a junior group open to boys and girls from ages ten to eighteen. Some time around 1960, the group ceased to be a vehicle for men's sports. Instead, from that point until after 2000 the group gave boys and girls a place to play baseball, softball, soccer, and basketball.

Fifty Years of Sporting Excellence—1944–1994: The C.S.M.A.C. Story was published by the Carondelet Sunday Morning Athletic Club in 1994. "The boys' parents did not have to be a member of C.S.M.A.C.," the book said of those eligible to join the junior group. "All the boys needed was his parents' approval and a dollar bill for his yearly dues. Ten cents a month was acceptable if a dollar was unavailable." That requirement also was waived, if necessary. "The dollar dues' only purpose was to provide the boy with a feeling of belonging." But over time, the club shrank as interest and volunteers declined and young people moved out of the area. In the end, a small group kept the gym open for bingo games that supported the club.

"We had one soccer team and one softball team, and we decided that we would close the doors," said Rich Meisemann, a longtime official of the group. "CSMAC served its purpose. We took care of kids when they couldn't afford to play sports." So in 2005, the club sold its gym building and its eleven acres of property at 1012 Loughborough to the developers of a new shopping center to be called the Loughborough Commons. The club is gone, but the CSMAC lives on in displays at the Carondelet Historical Society, 6303 Michigan Avenue, and in college scholarships from nearly $1 million the group received for the building. "We wanted to keep the name of CSMAC going, and we thought the best way to do that was to give scholarships," Meisemann said. In the five years after the group sold the building, it gave students in area high schools thirty scholarships for sports, academics, and community service worth nearly $300,000. Such is the end of a group that started by charging children a dime a month to play sports.

THE AMERICAN DREAM

Fati Dime is living the American dream. A refugee from Mauritania, she is building a life for herself at her Cisse's Fashion and Hair Braiding Salon at 4412 Chippewa Street. Like many others striving for the American dream, it comes with a cost. "I work twenty-four hours a day. You don't go anywhere. You just work," she said. "The good thing is if you work hard, you can get a lot of opportunities." Dime, who came to America in 2001, received help and training from the International Institute of St. Louis to set up her business.

The agency, which is based at 3654 South Grand Boulevard, has been helping immigrants and refugees adjust to life in St. Louis for more than ninety years. The group was founded in 1919 to help the flood of women who came to the St. Louis area primarily from European countries ravaged by World War I. Then as now, it offered services such as translation, English language classes, meeting medical needs, and helping people find employment. During World War II, the group helped relocate Japanese Americans from internment camps in the western United States. After the war, it started helping war brides from Japan and Europe. Since then, the focus has changed. In 1954, the agency offered the first citizenship classes in St. Louis to Japanese who were finally able to apply for U.S. citizenship after fifty-year-old restrictions were lifted. In the 1950s and 1960s, it worked with refugees fleeing from the failed Hungarian and Czechoslovakian revolutions. It helped to resettle Vietnamese refugees after the fall of Saigon in 1975 and Bosnians from 1993 to 2001. By the end of 2011, it will have sponsored twenty thousand refugees since 1975.

"We're sort of their welcome wagon," said agency President and CEO Anna Crosslin. The group picks up refugees at the airport, helps them find housing, teaches them English, and helps them find jobs. Many of them have since started businesses that have brought major changes to the South Side. She notes that a primary example of the effect of the agency's help on the community came after the International Institute moved to 3800 Park Avenue near Cardinal Glennon Hospital in 1982. Vietnamese clients who resettled south of the office along South Grand Boulevard noticed all the boarded-up buildings on South Grand. Others saw hopeless blight. The Vietnamese saw opportunity in an area with affordable rents. Soon they were opening businesses on South Grand. That was the start of the thriving international business district on South Grand south of Arsenal Street. Crosslin sees the same thing happening on Gravois Avenue in the Bevo Mill neighborhood, where Bosnians have brought new life to an area that once was devoid of promise.

Out of the approximately seventy thousand Bosnian refugees and their children now in the area, about half live in the city, Crosslin said. The International Institute resettled about seven thousand of them here, while Catholic Charities of the Archdiocese of St. Louis resettled several thousand more. "The anchor resettlements attracted friends and families who had been resettled in other states around the United States when they learned of the opportunities in St. Louis to find jobs and buy affordable homes. They flocked to our communities," Crosslin said. "It's a very typical pattern of immigrant waves throughout history."

Altogether, Crosslin estimates about ten percent of the city's population is made up of refugees. Without the help provided

THE INTERNATIONAL ✪ INSTITUTE ✪

by the International Institute, "They would basically be dropped in the middle of nowhere, as many of our grandparents and great-grandparents were in earlier generations," Crosslin said. "Instead, within a relatively short period of time—months, not years—most refugees adjust. They can be working, paying taxes, and on their way to integrating and becoming good neighbors, small business owners, and otherwise fully participating and contributing Americans." If anyone wonders how the South Side has turned around so much in recent years, a big reason has to be the hard work of refugees and immigrants. And the International Institute is a big reason why they've succeeded.

RAISE A GLASS

Few lovers of Budweiser, Bud Light, or Michelob have heard the name George Schneider, but perhaps they should raise a glass to him. If it wasn't for George Schneider, they might be drinking Coors or Miller instead. Who knows? In this alternate universe, Anheuser-Busch might be selling soap instead of beer. Schneider played a crucial role in the beginning of this most important of South Side companies. He was a brewer, but not a particularly successful one, which is a key to the story. He likely operated the Washington Brewery at 54 South 3rd Street in the 1840s and early 1850s, along with a beer garden and a saloon. In 1852, he opened the Bavarian Brewery on the east side of Carondelet Avenue (now South Broadway) between Dorcas and Lynch Streets. Soldiers at the nearby U.S. Arsenal provided a plentiful source of customers, so many, in fact, that the company moved to the west side of 8th Street, between Crittenden and Pestalozzi Streets in 1856. Then, perhaps because of the Panic of 1857, he started having money problems and sold his business. The new owners, Hammer & Urban, did well, but fell behind on loans. So in 1860, the firm transferred ownership to a major creditor: soap and candle manufacturer Eberhard Anheuser.

Anheuser and a friend, pharmacist William D'Oench, took over the brewery and renamed it the E. Anheuser and Company Bavarian Brewery. Anheuser recognized that while everybody needs soap, what the city's growing population of German immigrants really wanted was beer. He tried without success to manage his soap and beer business in tandem. Eventually, he sought out someone to manage his beer business. "Eberhard wanted a man who knew beer, who loved beer, and who could brew and sell beer," said the self-serving *Making Friends Is Our Business: 100 Years of Anheuser-Busch*, by Roland Krebs with Percy J. Orthwein. So he turned to his son-in-law, Adolphus Busch.

Adolphus was born July 10, 1839, in the Grand Duchy of Hesse and immigrated to the United States in 1857. "Having completed his education in Germany, and become a linguist of considerable skill, he went to America to seek his fortune," *Making Friends Is Our Business* claimed. He came to St. Louis and worked as a clerk in the wholesale supply business. Then he went into business with Ernst Wattenberg in the wholesale commission house of Wattenberg, Busch and Co. Somewhere along the line, possibly in business dealings with Anheuser, he met Eberhard's daughter, Lilly. Meanwhile, Adolphus's brother Ulrich met Lilly's sister Anna. On March 17, 1861, Adolphus married Lilly, and Ulrich married Anna, in a double wedding ceremony. "Adolphus was twenty minutes late for the ceremony," Peter Hernon and Terry Ganey wrote in *Under the Influence: The Unauthorized Story of the Anheuser-Busch Dynasty*. On his way to his wedding, he stopped to close a business deal.

After the wedding, Adolphus enlisted in the Union Army for three months. He returned to run his supply business and was taken into Anheuser's business as a partner in 1865. Soon he sold his interest in Wattenberg, Busch and Co. and bought D'Oench's share of the brewery. With the help of Adolphus, the company soon had to increase capacity to twenty-five thousand barrels. Adolphus was using all of his skills to sell his product. The beer was terrible, Hernon and Ganey wrote. To push it, Adolphus offered free beer to customers and payments to bar owners who stocked the beer. He also was early in using pasteurization to preserve the beer and ship it elsewhere.

His biggest innovation, however, was the King of Beers. Brewed with a process similar to the German pilsner beer, the Budweiser lager was introduced by E. Anheuser Co.'s Brewing Association in 1876. But there were problems. The bottler and distributor of the beer, C. Conrad and Co., registered the trademark for Budweiser in 1878. In 1883, Conrad filed for bankruptcy and licensed the name to what had become known as the Anheuser-Busch Brewing Association. In 1891, the brewery acquired all rights to the name in the United States, but disputes continue to this day. Budejovichy Budvar, which started brewing in 1895 in what is now the Czech Republic, also makes a beer called Budweiser. The Czech brewer disputes the rights to the name on the grounds that Budweiser is a style of beer based on the area it came from. Unquestionably, the product sold by Anheuser-Busch, or Anheuser-Busch InBev, since A-B was swallowed up in 2008, is the bigger seller.

RIVER STEAMERS DRIVEN FRO

EVENTS

WHEN THE GREAT FLOOD ALMOST BECAME THE GREAT FIRE

One hundred sixty-five years after the Great Fire of 1849, people still talk about the devastation it caused to the St. Louis riverfront. The fire killed at least three people and destroyed more than four hundred buildings on fifteen blocks. As bad as it was, though, a conflagration many times worse than that blaze almost came to the city's southern tip during the Great Flood of 1993. Neil Svetanics, the city's fire chief at the time, said a single spark could have ignited propane gas fumes that might have set ablaze a much larger section of far south St. Louis.

The source of that potentially deadly gas was a collection of liquid propane tanks kept by Phillips Petroleum at 8722 South Broadway, ready for Laclede Gas to use to give natural gas an extra kick during the winter heating season. The danger came from a network of pipes that connected one tank to another. If the water got too high, the pipes could start floating. The stress could cause them to leak dangerous amounts of propane. In South St. Louis, it was perhaps the scariest part of a flood that put the city's far southern tip and areas around the River des Peres under water.

Officials didn't worry about it at first. They thought the tanks could handle the predicted crest of forty-seven feet. To prepare, Phillips Petroleum filled the tanks to 85 percent of capacity and anchored them with three-quarter-inch thick steel cables. But the officials started sweating when the river level at St. Louis went over that forty-seven-feet line. By 10 A.M. on July 30, after the river had reached forty-eight feet, forty-eight of the fifty-one tanks started rising from their concrete cradles. "The tanks have gone up and down, flexing the pipe like a coat hanger," Svetanics said. It was time to act.

That day, all those within a half mile were evacuated. On August 1, the river at St. Louis reached a new high of 49.43 feet. It went down after the levee in Columbia, Illinois, burst. It meant disaster for farmers and people who lived along the bottomlands south of Columbia. But in South St. Louis and other places on the Mississippi River, it was as if somebody had pulled out the drain plug. "You could actually stand at the River des Peres and see the water go down," Svetanics said. "It sucked the water away from St. Louis, and the water dropped a foot or two." The water was dropping, but the danger was still there. After flash fires broke out on August 1, the evacuation area was expanded to a mile around the tanks on August 2. Altogether, nearly twelve thousand residents and owners had to leave. "They gave us three minutes to evacuate," said Evelyn Donovan, one of those evacuated on August 2. She grabbed medicine and a cane for her husband, Emmett Donovan, who was in the bathroom when police arrived and ordered them out of their house in the 7300 block of Pennsylvania Avenue.

Meanwhile, Svetanics offered a glimpse of the worst that could happen. A propane tank that was forced open would lose all of its propane in eleven seconds. From that one tank a cloud of gas would form, twelve feet deep and three thousand feet across. It would move along the ground until it found a spark setting off a massive explosion. To ease the situation, twenty divers from Phillips Petroleum prepared pipes so they would break off at a section and not at a tank valve where much more propane would be released. Svetanics and numerous other firefighters spent the time keeping a dangerously close watch on the situation.

Thankfully, the worst didn't happen. By August 6, business owners and residents within a mile were told they could go home. On August 11, after Phillips had removed all of the propane from the tanks, those within a half mile were given the go-ahead to return. At the end of the year, Phillips Petroleum reported it had paid $2 million to 6,252 people who made claims for food and lodging. The tank farm closed. Twenty-one years later, Svetanics reflected on the experience he had in the flood, including the near-explosion at Phillips Petroleum. "It was a heck of an experience. I don't think I'd want to go through it again, but I wouldn't have missed it for the world."

THE GRAND VIADUCT

A 1930 city map looks pretty much like a city map today, with a few exceptions. Among the differences in the 1930 map were the large tracts of undeveloped land in southwest St. Louis, particularly the part west of Hampton Avenue and south of Eichelberger Street. Development in South St. Louis was delayed primarily because of access to the rest of the city. South Siders could get downtown without much of a problem, but east-west railroads and the Mill Creek Valley made it harder for them to go north. "South Siders had this kind of separate identity from the rest of the city because they were isolated," said Mark Abbott, a Tower Grove South resident and a history professor specializing in urban topics at Harris-Stowe State University. This isolation during its formative years contributes to the area's unique character.

A change came in 1889, with the construction of the Grand Avenue Viaduct over the railroad tracks in the Mill Creek Valley. When it was built, the suspension bridge was considered one of the biggest of its kind: seven hundred feet long and sixty feet wide, with a thirty-six-foot roadway. The bridge, which was just north of Chouteau Avenue, looked like a smaller version of the Brooklyn Bridge, which was completed just six years earlier. As the Brooklyn Bridge connected Manhattan with Brooklyn, the Grand Avenue Viaduct connected the northern and southern parts of St. Louis. David R. Francis, who was then mayor, said it provided "additional modes of communication between those sections of the city separated by the Mill Creek Valley and its network of railroad yards." Francis thought the need was so great that he also wanted one to the east at 21st Street.

Francis didn't get what he wanted, but the Grand Avenue Viaduct nonetheless had a positive effect. "Until that bridge was built, very little development took place along that South Grand corridor either east or west," said Esley Hamilton, architectural historian for the St. Louis County Department of Parks and Recreation. In time, other north-south connections went up and the old ones became outdated. People complained the Grand Avenue Viaduct wasn't wide enough for all the traffic. In 1960, the old bridge was demolished, and an eighteen-month project started to replace it with a new six-lane roadway. To mark the occasion, the Landmarks Association of St. Louis placed a memorial wreath on the old viaduct. Landmarks president Gerhardt Kramer said the wreath was a symbol of regret that it had to be demolished. Kramer emphasized that his group didn't think the old rusty bridge should be preserved. "It is inadequate for present-day traffic," he said. By the time the viaduct became outdated, people well knew about the bottlenecks that a two-lane connector between the north and south caused, but nobody remembered what it was like when there were no connections at all.

THE GRAND AVENUE ✪VIADUCT✪

In terms of numbers, the killer tornado that roared through St. Louis and East St. Louis on May 27, 1896, was the third most deadly in American history. The monster twister killed 255 people, injured 1,000, and caused—adjusting for inflation—the greatest dollar amount of damage of any tornado in U.S. history. Starting near the current location of the St. Louis Psychiatric Rehabilitation Center on Arsenal Street, the twister struck the Missouri Botanical Garden and sped through Chouteau Avenue, Soulard, and south of downtown. The tornado damaged part of an approach to the Eads Bridge before crossing the river and sinking riverboats and destroying major parts of East St. Louis.

Builders got busy and repaired the damage, but one part of the South Side took well over seventy years to recover. Stately Lafayette Square already was in decline before the cyclone. The richest of St. Louis's rich, who had bought up homes around Lafayette Park after the Civil War, already were pushing further west toward Vandeventer Place, and later the Central West End, to escape the encroaching pollution of the city's factories.

Then came the killer tornado, which made a direct hit on Lafayette Park and the surrounding homes. Everywhere, trees were pulled up and made into splinters. The statues of George Washington and Thomas Hart Benton remained upright amidst the rubble. The Lafayette Park Presbyterian, Methodist, and Baptist churches were gutted, as was nearby City Hospital. The music pavilion, a favorite place to hear Strauss waltzes, was destroyed, along with numerous mansions. Charles Gibson, an early resident who served as solicitor general of the United States under President Abraham

THE GREAT of 1896 CYCLONE

Lincoln, said with tears that he easily could rebuild his home. But he would never live the decades it would take to restore the trees that were now gone from Lafayette Square.

Much of the damage was repaired, but the soul was gone from the place. Soon, the first of the beautiful homes around Lafayette Park were converted into rooming houses and sub-divided into multiple dwellings. Then, in 1923, the Missouri Supreme Court ruled unconstitutional a zoning law limiting property fronting the park to residences. Grocery stores and service stations went up in place of once-proud homes. Slum-lords and criminals took over.

Hope reinvigorated Lafayette Square. At the end of the 1960s, people who believed the former glory could return started buy-ing old property around the park and restoring it. They formed the Lafayette Square Restoration Committee in 1969 and held the first of what has become an annual house tour the next year. In 1972, the Board of Aldermen passed an ordinance making Lafay-ette Square the city's first historic district. It included limits on demolition of houses and strict restrictions meant to ensure that renovations met historic guidelines. The law provided protection for a new generation of urban pioneers. With their vision and work, Lafayette Square finally was over the Great Cyclone of 1896.

WHEN BEER FLOWED AGAIN

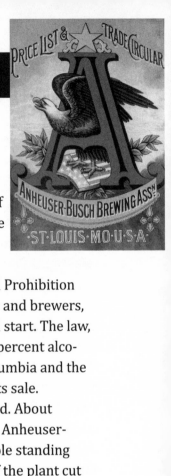

After thirteen long, dry years, South Siders raised the biggest glasses they could find after midnight on April 7, 1933. At nightclubs, restaurants, and watch parties, they tapped beer mugs filled high with 3.2 percent Budweiser and Falstaff and said to one and all, "Here's to ya" and "I'm sure glad that's over." Actually, Prohibition wasn't over. That would come on December 5, 1933, when passage of the Twenty-First Amendment repealed Prohibition for all forms of alcohol. But for local beer drinkers and brewers, the passage of the Cullen-Harrison Act was a good start. The law, which took effect April 7, legalized the sale of 3.2 percent alcohol by volume beer and wine in the District of Columbia and the twenty states in which state laws didn't prohibit its sale.

It was reason to celebrate, and South Siders did. About twenty-five thousand people crowded around the Anheuser-Busch plant at Broadway and Arsenal Street. People standing shoulder to shoulder on Pestalozzi Street north of the plant cut off traffic. Inside the brewery, Anheuser-Busch was preparing to ship forty-five thousand cases and eighteen thousand half-barrels right after it became legal. A brass band kept the crowd happy as they awaited the blowing of a whistle at midnight. "When the whistle blew, there was a deafening outburst of cheering," the *Globe-Democrat* said in that morning's edition. "Before the cheering subsided, the great doors of the bottling plant were lifted and the first trucks rolled out, the police clearing a way for them." Among the fifty-five trucks was a light truck under police escort with a case of beer for President Roosevelt and fifty-seven cases for other government officials. They headed for Lambert Field for a flight to Washington. The brewery had sixteen freight cars loaded on switching tracks. Trucks were lined up four blocks long. Meanwhile, a crowd estimated at ten thousand lined up at the Falstaff Brewery on Forest Park Boulevard.

At Anheuser-Busch, KMOX broadcast the words of Vice President August A. (Gussie) Busch Jr. in opening ceremonies after midnight. "April the 7th is here and it is a real occasion for thankfulness marking a newfound freedom for the American people made possible by the wisdom, foresight, and courage of a great president and the cooperation of an understanding Congress," Busch said. "Out of confusion and anxiety has grown a beacon light to guide the way to better times. Happy, grateful men are back at work after what seems an endless idleness."

The next day, as people recovered from their first legal binge in thirteen years, both Anheuser-Busch and Falstaff were overwhelmed with orders. Phone lines into both breweries were so tied up that it was impossible to get through. While upstarts like Blatz pushed their products in smaller ads, it was up to Falstaff and Anheuser-Busch to brag about themselves in full-page ads. "Prosit!" said a Falstaff ad. "Drink to this joyous advent, a beer of old, that always has been and is today the choicest product of the brewers' art." Anheuser-Busch claimed in its ads that not only was beer back, but its return also strengthened the economy. "Hands long idle find new jobs. Faces empty of hope brighten to a new promise. Thousands upon thousands find honorable employment." Indeed, some people did go back to work, but it was hardly enough to end the Depression. At least now, though, people could drink away their worries about the economy without worrying about being arrested.

It was a typically American story of boom and bust, and much of it played itself out on the South Side. In the 1950s and 1960s, St. Louis's Falstaff beer challenged Anheuser-Busch for dominance in the St. Louis market and became one of the leading brewers in the country. Then a slide began, and the company disappeared. So ended a tradition that began when the William J. Lemp Brewery, based at Lemp Avenue and Cherokee Street, introduced the brand at the start of the twentieth century. After the onset of Prohibition, the Lemp Brewery sold the company's trademark for twenty-five thousand dollars to a company organized by brewer Joseph Griesedieck and his son Alvin. It seemed foolish, but "Papa Joe" Griesedieck had no doubts. "He was convinced that eventually Prohibition would be repudiated by the American public and real beer would come back," Alvin Griesedieck wrote in his 1951 book, *The Falstaff Story*.

The Falstaff Corporation endured Prohibition by selling a nonalcoholic beer called Hek, along with other products like root beer, ham, and bacon. When Prohibition ended in 1933, Falstaff quenched thirsty beer drinkers throughout the country. The Falstaff Corporation received hundreds of applications from throughout the country from franchisers ready to sell the brew. The first truckloads moved out of a brewery at 3662–84 Forest Park Boulevard on April 7, 1933. That plant stayed open until 1958. In the South Side, another plant opened at the end of Prohibition at 3181 Michigan Avenue and remained open until 1952. A plant at 2000 Madison Street operated from 1948 to 1967. Meanwhile, Griesedieck Brothers Brewery, started by Joseph's brother Henry in 1911, also turned out Griesedieck Brothers beer from a brewery at Shenandoah and Lemp. The beer sponsored Cardinals games from 1944 to 1953, a time when Harry Caray first broadcast here. Falstaff merged with Griesedieck Brothers Brewery in 1957 and immediately killed production of that brand. It produced Falstaff at that plant from 1957 to 1977.

The merger was one of the moves that helped bring Falstaff close to the front of the brewing pack in the 1950s. By the end of the 1950s, Falstaff beer, "the Choicest Product of the Brewer's Art," was briefly the third most popular beer in America. In 1963, the *Globe-Democrat* reported on the busy life of Marie Olliges, who was responsible for furnishing Falstaff office buildings in eight different cities: St. Louis, Omaha, New Orleans, San Jose, Chicago, Fort Wayne, Galveston, and El Paso. The company had an impressive-looking headquarters at 5050 Oakland Avenue. It bragged about itself at the Falstaff Museum of Brewing in the Falstaff Inn at Shenandoah Avenue and Salena Street, near the brewery at Shenandoah and Lemp.

But the good times couldn't last. Production peaked in 1966 and then started to slide. In 1970, the company omitted a quarterly dividend to stockholders. In 1975, San Francisco businessman Paul Kalmanovitz bought the firm and moved its headquarters to San Francisco. The office at 5050 Oakland Avenue closed. Falstaff reintroduced Griesedieck Brothers beer briefly in the mid-1970s, but sales floundered. In 1977, the brewery on Shenandoah closed. Sales plummeted. The product was kept alive, but the company sold a mere 1,468 barrels in 2004. The next year, owner Pabst Brewing Company of San Antonio, turned off the tap on Falstaff for good. Today, the Saint Louis Science Center occupies the Oakland Avenue property where Falstaff had its headquarters. The site of the brewery on

Michigan Avenue now has a shuttered auto repair place on it. In 2006, a company announced plans to develop the old Falstaff Brewery at Lemp and Shenandoah as Falstaff Heights, complete with condominiums, stores, restaurants, and light industry. Nothing came of the plan, and the brewery is empty. A title loan company now occupies the old Falstaff Inn nearby.

In their book *St. Louis Brews: 200 Years of Brewing in St. Louis, 1809–2009*, Henry Herbst, Don Roussin, and Kevin Kious offer several reasons for Falstaff's demise. Among them were a change to a formula that the public didn't like and the age and inefficiency of the company's plants. A big money-draining loser was the Tapper, a small aluminum barrel that contained a case of beer. Each cost the company forty-eight dollars. The one-dollar deposit was hardly enough to persuade buyers to bring them back. "The bottom line is that Falstaff simply could not sell enough beer or limit production costs sufficiently to survive the beer wars that took place in the 1970s and beyond," *St. Louis Brews* claimed. For all of that, there are plenty of people who still hanker for one more drink of that choicest product, Falstaff.

It was the stuff you'd see in a 1950s crime flick. A perfectly planned bank robbery goes awry. Crowds of police officers and onlookers gather as terrified bank customers and employees crouch down to avoid the gunfire. When the shooting stops, a police officer is injured, two bank robbers are dead, and one robber is injured. The getaway car's driver eludes police but is quickly caught. In the best movie style, one robber takes his own life after declaring police would never take him alive. A police officer kills another robber as the thief rushes to the front door while using a woman as a shield. In fact, these sequences were the subject of a movie, based on actual events that occurred on April 24, 1953. The robbery at Southwest Bank at South Kingshighway Boulevard and Southwest Avenue was to become known as the Great St. Louis Bank Robbery.

The mastermind of the heist was Fred William Bowerman, described by the *Globe-Democrat* as a "lean, hard-eyed 'crime specialist' who was trading shots with police as far back as 1932." The year before, he was one of the robbers who shot a bank employee and got away with a total of $53,000 in the robbery of the National Bank and Trust Company of South Bend, Indiana. Now he was on the FBI's Ten Most Wanted List. Bowerman assembled his gang in Chicago and told members to "forget" their names and live apart from each other. That way, they couldn't tell police about the others if they were captured. Before the robbery, they met in Tower Grove Park to go over final details.

The robbery began at 10:15 on a payday Friday morning, when the bandits burst into the bank with cloths tied over the lower parts of their faces. One of them, holding a sawed-off shotgun and a brown zipper bag, jumped to a counter where he could see everybody in the bank. "This is a holdup. Everybody stand still," he shouted. He turned to the tellers and said, "Come out of those cages and get down on the floor." In another part of the building, the bank's directors were in their weekly meeting.

GIVE TO THE
BOY SCOUT
CAMPAIGN

Vol. 78—No. 318—Section A

St. Louis Gl

Over One Hund

St. Louis Saturday Morning,

POLICE FOIL $141

One Bandit Kills Himself; T

Hearing the commotion, bank president Dillon J. Ross called the switchboard operator who was working in the basement and told her to call the police. Meanwhile, a teller pressed a button under a counter alerting authorities.

Corporal Robert Heinz and Patrolman Melburn Stein were quick to respond. The robbers answered Stein's shots with gunfire. Heinz was shot in his ear and neck. Soon police from throughout the city were on the scene. As customers and bank employees cowered on the floor, police tossed tear gas canisters through the bank's windows. Bowerman grabbed Eva Hamilton and pressed his sawed-off shotgun against her back. "Don't shoot, or I'll kill her," he said. Undeterred, Stein aimed from the hip and felled the bandit. Bowerman later died from his wounds. "I felt sure I could get him by shooting from the hip and not harm the woman," Stein later said. "I had eight years of training in the Marine Corps in shooting from the hip." The game was up, and robber Frank Vito knew it. "They're not going to get me. I'll kill myself first," he said. He put a pistol to his head and shot himself. Another robber, William Scholl, grabbed bank customer Gloria Cantino. "Don't shoot. I've got a baby at home," she pleaded. "Don't worry, lady, I won't e-**Democrat.**

"GET ACTION TODAY"
on Your Want Ad
DIAL GA. 1212
The Result Number

ars Old This Year

1953—3 Sections—28 Pages

FIVE CENTS | IN GREATER ST. LOUIS | TEN CENTS ELSEWHERE

00 BANK HOLDUP

Others and Policeman Shot

hurt you. I've got children of my own," Scholl responded. Wounded by a shot fired by police, Scholl gave himself up at Cantino's urging. Several days later, police arrested the driver of the getaway car, former Marquette University football player Glenn Chernick, in Chicago. On the floor of the bank, police found a bag the robbers had stuffed with nearly $141,000. Chernick and Scholl later were sentenced to twenty-five years in prison.

St. Louis police received praise from throughout the country for the way they'd foiled the robbery. One of the policemen, Melburn Stein, had a chance to show the world how he did it, by playing himself in a movie about the heist called *The Great St. Louis Bank Robbery*. The 1959 movie starred a new actor named Steve McQueen. The director was Charles Guggenheim, who went on to win three Academy Awards for his documentaries. The movie featured shots of Southwest Bank and other South Side locations. But it's not a travelogue. Those and other scenes are shot in a gloomy black and white that befits a tale of a sad group of criminals about to do something stupid. McQueen wasn't yet the actor who rode a motorcycle in *The Great Escape*, but he did show promise as a college dropout showing doubts about the robbery plan.

Southtown Famous brought class to the South Side. Long before Macy's bought the parent company of Famous-Barr, the department store was the city's equivalent of Macy's. After Famous opened a $3.25 million branch at Chippewa Street and Kingshighway Boulevard on August 24, 1951, South Side families didn't have to take the Chevy or the bus downtown to buy fancy suits and dresses they saw advertised in the paper.

The store opened to big fanfare. Fifteen thousand people showed up to watch Mayor Joseph M. Darst use specially made sterling silver scissors to cut the ribbon opening the store. Seven-year-old Patricia and nine-year-old Susan Feiner, granddaughters of Famous-Barr vice president Fred Z. Salomon, dressed in navy blue and white polka dot costumes to hold the ribbon for the mayor to cut. Explorers and Boy Scouts from Troop 115 at nearby St. Mary Magdalen Church provided the color guard. A crew from KSD-TV (now KSDK-TV) showed up to film the event for the six o'clock news. Darst spoke with enthusiasm about the store's possibilities. "I believe this beautiful structure signifies the confidence held by business leaders throughout the nation in the people of St. Louis," the *Globe-Democrat* quoted him as saying. "Here we have an outstanding example of this company's recognition of the economic possibilities to be developed in St. Louis." The crowd was so big that twice in the first twenty minutes after the doors opened store officials asked the police to close them.

The next day, the *Globe-Democrat* quoted Morton D. May, Famous-Barr general manager and president of May Department Stores Company, on the importance of the store. He said the company's growth was closely connected with the expansion of the city. He spoke of the enormous development of the south and west parts of the city, which the store would serve. The store actually was the second Famous-Barr opened outside downtown. The first was in Clayton. But what the Southtown Famous had to offer made up for the fact that it wasn't first. Shoppers could choose from 150 different departments. Two thousand cars could fit into fifteen acres of parking lots. Motorists who parked in a lot across Chippewa Street could enter the store through a tunnel leading under the busy road. Not wanting to waste any chances, the store lined the tunnel with kiosks.

In 1959, shoppers could view new gas appliances in a seven-room landscaped house in a parking lot called the "Blue Flame Home." A beer garden went up in 1966. Until the early 1970s, people filled the tunnel before the store opened on the last

Thursday of every month to be the first inside for the "Dollar Day" promotion. Frank Scheithauer, a South Sider and a long-time Southtown display manager, noted in a 1995 article in the *South Side Journal* that window displays changed every two weeks. "We were real elaborate with the windows," he said. "It took a day and a half at the most to do one window, but sometimes we had to do three or four in a day."

It was a place to make memories, but it couldn't last. Faced with a loss of customers, Famous-Barr closed the store in January 1992. Plans were to replace it with a new Home Quarters mega hardware store. Nothing came of that, and a wide coalition of neighborhood groups fought plans to put a K-Mart in its place. They won, and a combination of small and big stores opened at the location in the mid-2000s as the Southtown Centre. The center, which includes such stores as Starbucks, PetSmart, Walgreens, and OfficeMax, is one of a number of shopping areas that are thriving on the South Side. They include Target, Hampton Village, Loughborough Commons, the South Grand international business district, and a number of smaller neighborhood shopping districts.

As the city slept early the morning of February 10, 1959, a deadly beast prepared to pounce. At Lambert–St. Louis Airport, meteorologists read their thermometers and barometers and saw something was wrong. The temperature dropped while air pressure spiked. Earlier, they had warned of severe thunderstorms, but nothing more. A squall line had developed about eight to ten miles long, moving about sixty miles ahead of a cold front going east at about thirty to thirty-five miles an hour. Then it happened. "Apparently the frontal cloud touched down and made contact," Weather Bureau meteorologist Leon Greninger told the *Post-Dispatch* later.

That's the way a meteorologist would say that the third most deadly tornado in St. Louis history met the earth around 1:40 A.M. at Manchester Avenue and Brentwood Boulevard and roared northeast. The 694-foot tower of KTVI–Channel 2 at 5915 Berthold Avenue crumbled and fell onto the nearby Arena parking lot and a four-family apartment. The twister then punched a hole in the roof of the Arena, demolished the Old Barn's east ornamental tower, and destroyed nearby homes. Then it crossed Highway 40 and exacted deadly tolls on neighborhoods between Kingshighway and Grand Boulevards. As the storm moved on, Cardinals first baseman Joe Cunningham was discussing a Bible verse with a buddy at his apartment at 4255 Olive Street when they heard a roar. "I jumped from my chair and ran into the next room and just then the ceiling caved

THE GREAT of 1959 TORNADO

in where I had been sitting. I crouched in a corner of the next room until we could make our way to the street," he said. While he thanked God for sparing his life, the tornado sputtered out around 2:15 A.M. near the McKinley Bridge. Twenty-one people were dead and 354 injured. The *Globe-Democrat* estimated that four thousand buildings were damaged.

It was deadly, and the Weather Bureau missed it. It didn't issue a special bulletin about a tornado until 3:30 A.M. Sheepishly, the bureau, the forerunner of the National Weather Service, contended it didn't issue a warning because the twister was an isolated case that couldn't be pinpointed. Even if it had predicted the tornado, it couldn't have gotten the word out at that late hour; the bureau contended nobody had made arrangements to use the civil defense siren system for that purpose. Meanwhile, the city's civil defense office didn't start work until three hours after the tornado struck. "I grant you the way it did work was all wrong," retired Brigadier General Francis P. Harding, the city's civil defense director, said. However, the civil defense operation responded enough that Mayor Raymond Tucker praised it for its work after the initial delay. After the deadly tornado in 1927, it would have taken twenty-four to thirty-six hours to organize a disaster response, he said.

Others responded quickly. Overwhelmed by the carnage, the city's hospitals met the challenge. Homer G. Phillips Hospital, located near the worst of the carnage, did well by following a disaster plan it had previously rehearsed. The American Red Cross set up four shelters for storm victims. Within hours, President Dwight D. Eisenhower declared St. Louis a major disaster area, making it eligible for federal relief funds. And TV watchers who worried they might not see episodes of *Maverick* and *77 Sunset Strip* were relieved to learn Channel 2 was back on the air with a weak signal by 4 P.M. Meanwhile, the *Globe-Democrat* tried to calculate when the next big tornado would strike. Major twisters killed 255 people in 1896, 76 in 1927, and 21 in 1959, coming at the rate of once every 31 or 32 years. By that logic, the next giant twister should have been in 1990. It hasn't arrived yet.

THE INTRUDING INTERSTATES

Dwight Eisenhower wreaked havoc, first as a general moving his armies across France and Germany and then as the president who established the Interstate Highway System. Both actions did good, but at a cost. When two interstates came to the South Side, they ended traffic snarls and made it faster to get from downtown to Arnold or Kirkwood. But people who had lived in their homes for decades were uprooted and made to live elsewhere. Neighborhoods were split. If the new Interstates 44 and 55 quickly brought people into the city from Fenton and South County, they also made it easier for city residents to move away. Many did. What happened with the interstates here and elsewhere was an example of the law of unintended consequences.

South Siders first heard of the highways after Eisenhower signed the Federal Aid Highway Act of 1956. In October 1957, news came of plans to spend $47 million on a 15.4-mile I-55 from the Meramec River through South County and into the South Side. Then, in 1960, the Missouri Highway Department announced a route for Interstate 44 that generally followed its current path, including through the Hill neighborhood. It didn't make two powerful Hill neighborhood politicians happy. State Representative Paul M. Berra complained the route was two miles longer than other proposed routes. Twenty-Fourth Ward alderman Anthony Mascazzini contended that the route wouldn't serve the most people. "The route chosen will bring traffic congestion to our ward and to every ward east of us," he said.

As people in the path of I-44 worried, the state started buying property in the path of I-55. An early victim was Cherokee Cave at 3400 South Broadway, which once was used by the old Lemp Brewery to keep beer cool. The historic Chatillon-DeMenil Mansion on the same property was saved when the path of the interstate was moved east. The Landmarks Association of

St. Louis persuaded Union Electric (now Ameren) to buy the mansion from the state. Another historic mansion wasn't as fortunate. The Philip Medart House at 1729 Missouri Avenue was sold to the State Highway Commission to make way for I-44. The mansion was built in 1890 by Philip Medart, who was an officer in the Union forces in the Civil War. He later patented a number of inventions, including mechanical devices and pulleys. Another historic house on the same block, the Carl Daenzer Mansion, also was sacrificed for Interstate 44. Daenzer was a prominent German immigrant journalist in St. Louis in the last half of the nineteenth century.

Even where historic houses weren't sacrificed, there were reasons to worry. In 1965, years before I-44 construction started in their area, people living around Tower Grove Park and the Missouri Botanical Garden expressed concern about what was happening in areas the state had bought. In some sections, the state tore down buildings without clearing away rubble. In other sections, people were allowing their property to deteriorate because they knew the state would buy it. Property bought by the state stayed vacant for months. That way, the state could tear down whole groups of buildings. It was good for the state budget, but not good for neighborhoods.

In the Hill neighborhood, loud and persistent protests forced the builders of I-44 to change their plans not once but twice. They first focused on an interchange planned for Macklind Avenue and I-44. That was too much for Hill residents, who worried the project would take about a third of the popular Berra Park at Macklind and Shaw Avenues and remove nine or ten more houses. The neighbors organized trips to the state capital to protest the plans. Before long, the interchange was dropped from the plans for the interstate, but Hill residents weren't done. In the early 1970s, concerned that some Hill residents north of the interstate would be cut off from the rest of the neighborhood, they fought for another bridge across the highway just east of the Macklind Avenue Bridge. Hundreds turned out at meetings on the Hill and in Jefferson City to press their case. Neighbors even called on television personality Joe Garagiola, who grew up on the Hill, to intervene on their behalf with his friend, U.S. Secretary of Transportation John Volpe. In the end, the pressure paid off. Hill residents got their Edwards Street Overpass. "It shows organizational skill. It shows the very fact that people were determined," said Monsignor Salvatore Polizzi. At the time, he was assistant pastor of the Hill's St. Ambrose Catholic Church and a key leader of the neighborhood's fights over I-44. Their efforts reduced the effect of those projects, but the construction of I-44 and I-55 on the South Side changed neighborhoods forever.

It was the Six Flags of its time, and it burned on a hot summer day. The blaze that destroyed the Forest Park Highlands was nearly a half century ago, but those who remember its passing still grieve for it as the end of a precious childhood memory. They think of the pool they swam in during school picnics, the carousel, the rocket ship, the fun houses, the train, and the kisses they stole from their dates on the Ferris wheel. The amusement park in the 5600 block of Oakland Avenue was a place for making such memories after the Highlands Cottage Restaurant opened there in 1896. A merry-go-round soon went up, followed by nine other rides. School children took the streetcar to the Highlands and delighted in the ever-expanding amusement park.

Over the years, local boxers had a chance to try their skill against traveling champion boxers such as Jack Dempsey and "Gentleman Jim" Corbett. John Philip Sousa directed his band at the Highlands, and stars such as Eddie Howard, Harry James, Tommy Dorsey, Marie Dressler, and Sophie Tucker entertained. At one time, one hundred schools a year booked picnics at the park. Sandy Honaker of Wentzville remembers going to the Highlands when she attended Epiphany of Our Lord School at 6576 Smiley Avenue. "Our school picnics were held at the Highlands. That was a big exciting treat," said Honaker, who lived near present-day Interstate 44 and Arsenal Street until she was eighteen. She recalls "the old wooden roller coasters and all the rides. That was really fun."

People loved the place, but in the early 1960s, the Junior College District, now the St. Louis Community College, coveted the fourteen-acre property for a campus. Rumors spread that 1963 would be the Highlands' last year. While folks were discussing what might happen with the Highlands, a fire settled the matter. Around 2:30 P.M. on July 19, 1963, a fire broke out in the basement of the building housing the restaurant, concession stands, and dance hall. The flames quickly spread, but by 3 P.M., firefighters thought the fire was under control. Winds, however, kicked up to fifteen to twenty miles an hour. Soon there was nothing firefighters could do. "All the water in the world wouldn't put that out," Assistant Fire Chief Robert Olsen said. "It makes a man feel small and insignificant to watch something like this and to be helpless no matter how many big pieces of equipment you have." The heavy black smoke and fire rose as high as 100 to 150 feet and could be seen for miles.

When the fire was over, only the roller coaster, Ferris wheel, and carousel survived among the rides. "It was sad. Then we had to take the bus all the way up to the Chain of Rocks for our school picnics," Honaker said. She referred to the old Chain of Rocks Amusement Park near the old Chain of Rocks Bridge. Speculation was that careless smoking or faulty wiring was the cause, but nobody knew for sure. Part of what is now St. Louis Community College at Forest Park went up on the park property. A question turned up at local trivia nights: "Where did the carousel from the Forest Park Highlands wind up?" Answer: St. Louis County's Faust Park. *St. Louis Post-Dispatch* writer Theodore P. Wagner noted another memory of the park: "Fire spectators observed that the illuminated Star Spangled Banner, high above the park, appeared and reappeared through black clouds of smoke like the flag of a ship sinking with colors flying." Like the original Star Spangled Banner, this one remained when the last of the fire was out.

THE *FOREST PARK HIGHLANDS*

THE IRISH GO TO THE DOGS

A full-blooded Irishman, Bob Corbett has extra reasons to smile every St. Patrick's Day. Since the mid-1990s, Corbett has lived in the house he grew up in on Tamm Avenue in Dogtown. By coincidence or not, that gave him the perfect view of the annual St. Patrick's Day Parade of the Ancient Order of Hibernians. For nearly a quarter century, the parade has passed in front of his house. The St. Louis City and St. Louis County boards of the Hibernians first held the parade in Clayton on March 17, 1984. Unfortunately, the next year Clayton insisted on holding it on a Saturday, even though March 17 that year was on a Sunday. So the parade in 1985 was held on March 17, but on Howdershell Road in Hazelwood. Finally, the Hibernians decided to move the parade to Dogtown, which has long had a reputation of being the last traditional Irish neighborhood in St. Louis.

It's not quite true to say Dogtown is an Irish neighborhood, Corbett said. Then again, he adds, it's sort of true. Since around the time he moved into the home he grew up in, the retired philosophy professor at Webster University has become his neighborhood's leading historian. A curious type, he decided the idea that Dogtown was and is an Irish neighborhood should be tested. He looked at all census records from 1900 for people who lived in present-day Dogtown—from Oakland Avenue to Interstate 44 and Macklind to McCausland Avenues.

"It turns out that the Irish were not even the dominant minority," Corbett said. Germans outnumbered Irish by about twenty. The Irish outnumbered French by about twenty. Others who followed included English and Croatians. But these numbers don't mean the place wasn't Irish. The dominant social organization of the area was St. James the Greater Catholic Church, which started around 1860 after miners and brick makers started coming to the area in the late 1850s. For ninety-two years, from the time the church started in 1860 to 1952, the church's pastors were born, educated, and ordained in Ireland.

They came to the church as missionary priests, and all made their mark. The last of those Irish pastors, Father Patrick J. O'Connor, wrote about them in his 1937 book, *History of*

Cheltenham and St. James Parish. He served forty years at the church, from 1912 until his death in 1952. The church's first pastor, Father John O'Sullivan, who served from 1860 to 1861, was a "hot and outspoken secessionist." Father Thomas Manning, who served from May 1869 to January 31, 1870, left the parish suddenly and was reported to be insane. The most revered and loved of the early pastors was Father Henry Kelly, who served from 1870 to 1878. Of the Reverend Edmond Casey, who was pastor from 1896 to 1916, O'Connor wrote, "He was by no means an ascetic and he was rarely suspected of being saintly, but he prayed with the confidence of a bad little boy that right away forgot and was mischievous." O'Connor also wrote that "His laughter was loud and contagious, his sympathy was deep and tear drops came as quickly to his eye as to a woman's." O'Connor could speak with experience about Casey, since he served under him for four years before he took over the parish.

Those priests were different but were all united in faith and nationality. As Corbett sees it, the uneducated miners and brick makers relied on those priests to teach them how to behave. In response, the priests taught them how to live in an Irish village. "It became Irish culturally, although it was not ethnically. It's maintained a great deal of that today," Corbett said. As for what goes by his house every St. Patrick's Day, he said, "I'm delighted with the parade, utterly totally delighted. Best day of the year."

Father O'Connor poses with children from St. James Parish.

AN EXORCISM

At hospitals, doctors try to use the science they have learned to cure diseases of the body and mind, but people say something profoundly unscientific happened in 1949 in the since-demolished psychiatric wing of Alexian Brothers Hospital at 3933 South Broadway. There, the accounts say, priests performed a full-blown exorcism on a fourteen-year-old boy, complete with weird noises and flying things. The events at the institution now called St. Alexius Hospital later became the basis of a 1971 novel, *The Exorcist*, and an Oscar-winning movie of the same name in 1973. William Peter Blatty, author of both the novel and the screenplay, learned about the exorcism after reading a three-paragraph news article. Blatty, who also wrote scripts for director Blake Edwards, made the person who was exorcised a twelve-year-old girl and located the event in Mount Rainier, Maryland, a suburb of Washington, D.C. His account, including a description of the possessed girl as "a cursing, vomiting, convulsive, murdering monster," led many critics and Catholics to call *The Exorcist* exploitative and harmful.

The real event was scary enough, if the accounts are to be believed. Early in 1949, the fourteen-year-old boy and his grandmother started hearing odd scratching noises for several hours each night in a home in Mount Rainier. About a month later, scratches were seen on the boy's body. Then words began to appear in the scratches. The family, which was Lutheran, asked for help from a Lutheran minister. The Lutheran minister asked for help from a priest. Two priests were injured in an attempt to exorcise the boy at Georgetown University Hospital. One, the Reverend Albert E. Hughes, lost full use of his arm when the boy slashed his right arm with a piece of bedspring. He broke the nose of a second, the Reverend Walter H. Halloran. The boy then was moved to St. Louis where his mother had an uncle and an aunt. The boy wound up at Alexian Brothers, where the Reverend William S. Bowdern, pastor of St. Francis Xavier Church at St. Louis University, was named to lead the exorcism. Others present who assisted were the Reverend William Van Roo and Halloran.

The Reverend Raymond Bishop described the events in detail in a twenty-six-page diary. That diary provided much of the basis for Thomas B. Allen's 1993 book about the events, *Possessed: The True Story of an Exorcism*. Halloran talked about it in a 1988 newspaper interview. "The little boy would go into a seizure and get quite violent," Halloran said. "So Father Bowdern asked me to hold him." The priest also contended arrows, streaks, and words such as "hell" appeared on the child's skin. The story was kept quiet for years, but rumors led St. Louis cardinal Joseph Ritter to order a Jesuit examiner to conduct an investigation. The investigator concluded demonic possession wasn't involved, but a "psychosomatic disorder and some kinesis action that we do not understand but which is not necessarily preternatural."

Bowdern, meanwhile, never acknowledged his role in the exorcism but confided to friends he believed it was a bona fide incident of possession. Mickey McTague, a Catholic and well-known local figure who has made a long study of the events at Alexian Brothers Hospital, agrees with Bowdern. McTague's father was a close friend of Dr. Ed Sassin, who was chief of psychiatry at Alexian Brothers at the time of the exorcism. McTague, who was nine at the time, remembers Sassin talking about the events when he visited the McTague home at 3128 Allen Avenue in Compton Heights. Almost all of the nearly fifty witnesses to the event believed demonic activity was involved, McTague said. What they saw convinced them that something happened at Alexian Brothers that science could not explain.

UNUSUAL, UNIQUE, OR JUST PLAIN ODD

A BRAINY PLACE TO EAT

Customers said the fried chicken at Ferguson's Pub was better than Hodak's. But that's not what made the place at 2925 Mount Pleasant Street stand out. The brains of the operation did. No, that's not Billie Ferguson, who became the bar's owner after her husband John died in January 2010. She was smart too, but it was the fried beef brains served on rye bread with pickles, onions, chips, and horseradish sauce that brought people all the way from Potosi. A man who lived in the area moved to Washington, D.C., and came back for a visit. He asked for forty of the brain patties—hold the bread, thank you. He put them in dry ice and brought them to Washington, where they don't have brains.

"They taste like scrambled eggs or liver. They're really bland, really mild," the red-haired Ferguson said. They tasted like chicken to her son Steve. They looked sort of like a breaded pork cutlet and long were served at a few eateries on the South Side. But they were part of a dying breed when a visitor dropped by in 2010. They were on the menu at Ferguson's ever since Billie and John opened the restaurant on St. Patrick's Day in 1980. There had been a bar at the same place for thirty years before that. "When we bought this, they still walked in and bought those buckets of beer," Ferguson said.

At Ferguson's Pub, a huge mirror was behind the bar, and red-and-white plaid plastic tablecloths were on the tables. A big framed picture of Mark McGwire smacking a home run was among the items on the wall honoring the Cardinals. There were numerous signs for Anheuser-Busch products, which helped wash down many of the fifty or so brain sandwiches sold at the pub each month. Customer John Dennis had one once. "I thought it was OK until I got to the middle. It's not for me," Dennis said. "I didn't feel smarter." A customer who only gave his first name—Brian—said they made the best brain sandwiches at Ferguson's. "I'm going by hearsay," he said. Barb Gannon, a waitress at the place, wouldn't go near the stuff.

Nobody's going to experience the taste of a brain sandwich any more, at least not at 2925 Mount Pleasant Street. Ferguson sold the place to Lance Lindner in 2012. She died shortly before he finished renovations and reopened the place in June 2013 as Lindner's Pub. His menu doesn't include brain sandwiches. "When it comes to brain sandwiches, there's a lot of prep time," Lindner said. One place that still offers it is Schottzie's Bar and Grill, 11428 Concord Village Avenue in south St. Louis County. The future may not be bright for brain sandwiches. Time will tell whether that's a smart idea.

THE BRAIN SANDWICH

A mistake in the kitchen more than sixty years ago may have led to a Hill neighborhood specialty that's as much a part of St. Louis's culinary sphere as pork steaks, Gus' Pretzels, and gooey butter cake. The deep-fried delight, however, has origins shrouded in mystery. Mickey Garagiola, brother of broadcaster Joe Garagiola, contends the mistake happened at Oldani's Tavern, which today is Mama Campisi's Restaurant at 2132 Edwards Street. According to Mickey, some time in the late 1940s an inebriated bartender took an order of ravioli and dropped it in boiling oil instead of boiling water. Rather than waste it, the bar's owner had it served to customers with cheese and red sauce. Garagiola claims he was there after spending the night as a waiter at Ruggeri's Restaurant and saw the new creation brought out. The customers loved it so much that the owner put it on the menu. "Everybody claimed to be the original," Garagiola said. "The original was down in Oldani's." Most today seem to agree with him.

But wait. Some say it happened at Charlie Gitto's, at 5226 Shaw Avenue on the Hill, when it was Angelo's Restaurant. In this telling, a woman was startled and accidentally dropped ravioli in boiling oil. After it was retrieved, it tasted delicious. The origin claims can continue, but all the creation stories share a common theme: toasted ravioli was an accident. Unless it wasn't. After all, gooey butter cake was also supposedly invented by accident. The truth is, nobody knows, which is just as well. It's enough to say the new creation gradually took hold in the neighborhood and became a St. Louis specialty, but

*T*OASTED

*R*AVIOLI

it never caught on nationally. Joseph R. DeGregorio, who gives guided tours of the Hill, said that people on his tours who come from farther away than 150 miles generally don't know about toasted ravioli. He brings tour groups to Mama Toscano's Ravioli at 2201 Macklind Avenue. In its handmade method, a filling of pork, beef, spinach, onions, carrots, and tomatoes is poured on dough. Then another layer of dough is placed on top. Next, a specially made roller with square indentations is rolled over the mix, stamping out ravioli either for toasting or boiling. After being cut apart, ravioli for toasting is washed with eggs and milk, dipped in breadcrumbs, and frozen. Later, the raviolis are placed in a skillet and fried briefly on either side, preferably with canola oil. Then they are sprinkled with cheese and served with marinara sauce. Other makers produce their toasted ravioli by machine, which results in ridges and a crustier and harder dough. Some restaurants buy toasted ravioli from Mama Toscano's or other places. Others make their own. However they make it, people still are thankful to whoever dropped the ravioli in the wrong pan.

THE SOUTH SIDE SHOTGUN

Gina Meyer loves her house, and she loves the location on the Hill. Besides, it's down the street from Milo's Tavern at 5201 Wilson Avenue, where she tends bar. But there are disadvantages, beginning with the fact that the house is only fourteen and a half feet wide. Anybody who wants to go from the small living room to the dining room, kitchen, and bathroom has to pass through her bedroom. It makes it hard to entertain, she said. Her two daughters live in converted bedrooms in the basement. Things could be worse, though. The kitchen and dining areas originally were in the basement. "I guess it beats an apartment," Meyer said.

Meyer lives in a shotgun house, so named because it is so narrow that a person could shoot a shotgun in the front of the house and see the shot pass through the back. Generally, they don't have hallways. These houses are plentiful on the Hill. The homes began with Italian immigrants who arrived here between 1890 and 1904, said Joseph R. DeGregorio, a second-generation tour guide on the Hill. They lived in shantytowns and boarding-houses while they saved their money to bring their loved ones to America. With the close of the 1904 World's Fair, the opportunity came for them to move into something better. All of the structures at the fair had to be dismantled. "There was a lot of free lumber to be had from all those dismantled buildings," DeGregorio said. So they began building homes near the Italian missionary church at Wilson and Marconi Avenues, near the present site of St. Ambrose Church. These homes were in the shotgun style, since it allowed people to build more homes in a given block. Bricks and concrete later were added to many, along with a second floor to some. Kitchens often were put in the basement, and many of the homes still have kitchens there. Many of the front lawns were small with elongated backyards. They had long gardens in the back. Only a couple of shotgun house owners have added a second floor, DeGregorio said, but some of the homes are actually classified as two-story because the basement is at street level. Many of the shotgun homes were built on stilts as the basements were filled in later when the owner had the money.

In the spring of 2010, Hill real estate agent Carol Savio was showing a shotgun house in the 5200 block of Botanical Avenue. At twenty feet wide, it was not quite as narrow as Meyer's, but there were distinct signs that this home was built in the shotgun style. The outhouse was in the back. As with many shotgun homes, the kitchen originally was in the basement. The kitchen and bathroom were added on to the back of the house. "People just kept adding on and on," Savio said. Originally, people would have walked into the living room, then the first bedroom, and then the second one. In this house, as in all shotgun houses, people have done work to modernize them.

While shotgun houses are typically associated with the Hill, they are common throughout the South Side. One of them is not far from the Bevo Mill. Ryan Calaway lives in a fifteen-foot-wide frame shotgun house with his two-and-a-half-year-old daughter, Tristin. It looks uncomfortably small on the outside. But on the inside, it is surprisingly spacious. "It's a tiny house, but for the two of us, we're not too crowded," said Calaway. An open kitchen is behind the living room. Calaway and his daughter live in the bedroom behind that. "I don't know that I would stay here forever, but really, it's been ideal for the last five or six years of my life." He paid $59,500 for it at the height of the real estate bubble and got back a $5,000 rebate for rehab work. It may be high in 2010 dollars, but it's still one of the lowest prices around for a house. With Calaway and other buyers of shotgun houses, that's the biggest attraction.

PRETZEL MEN

A gaunt man with a graying beard and a ponytail looks at northbound motorists who have just exited Interstate 55 and are preparing to turn left onto Loughborough Avenue. Then a woman motions to him. She gives him five dollars. In return, he gives her six pretzel sticks individually bagged so they are not soiled by his hands. "Ain't too much to smile about. It don't look like I'm going to make forty dollars today," Charles Boyd said. On a good night, he can make forty dollars between 4 P.M. and 7 P.M. after deducting his costs. But this wasn't a good night. He bought the pretzels for twenty-five cents each from Gus' Pretzels store at 1820 Arsenal Street. "I made more money panhandling this corner than I did selling pretzels," Boyd said. One reason is the vendors license Boyd wore around his neck. It set him back two hundred dollars. He also had to sign up to pay sales tax. Otherwise a cop might see him and haul him in.

Once, people like Boyd sold pretzels everywhere on South Side street corners. Gus Koebbe Jr., who owns Gus' Pretzels, said one reason for the change is laws that make it more difficult for people just to go buy pretzels and start selling them. Those include restrictions on where they can sell and vendors licenses. "Now, a lot of people don't want to be standing on the street corners," he said. He estimates about a half-dozen people buy from him. But big profits still are possible. Street vendors buy anywhere from fifty to five hundred pretzels and sell them for a dollar each. On Loughborough, Jamieson Avenue, and Hampton Avenue, there are much fewer pretzel sellers than there once were, but those who look will still find them.

Koebbe knows what the pretzel vendor goes through. He easily could have made enough for soda and candy by selling newspapers, but his father—Gus Koebbe Sr.—wouldn't hear of it. After all, Gus Sr. was the second generation in the family business known then and now as Gus' Pretzels. So Gus' father gave him a supply of stick pretzels and sent him out to sell them. Back in 1964, when Koebbe was eight, pretzels wholesaled for two and a half cents and retailed for a nickel. Today, they're a quarter in lots of one hundred or more.

He found plenty of takers among people building an Arsenal Street bridge over the new Interstate 55. At a high school football game, he could sell five hundred pretzels in two and a half hours. Koebbe, who stopped selling when he went into high school, didn't do as well at some street corners. Sometimes it would take him four or five hours to sell a couple of hundred at a slow corner. Bit it was still enough to keep him in pocket money.

The tradition of selling pretzels on the street enabled Koebbe's grandfather, Frank Ramsperger, to make a living after he lost the use of an eye in an accident at his job as a riveter. He started baking pretzels. "Back in those days, you could make stuff at your home and go sell it at the corner," Koebbe said. Eventually, he got a shop. In 1942, Koebbe's grandfather bought the building where the pretzels are now made. Ten years later, Koebbe's father and mother bought the business and gave it the current name. Today, under the leadership of Gus Jr., the company makes about forty-eight to fifty thousand pretzels a week. "We go through a couple hundred sacks of flour a week," Koebbe said. Many of the finished products go into stores around the area. Besides regular pretzels, people who come to Gus' Pretzels can buy cinnamon sugar pretzels, garlic pretzels, and salsiccia, bratwurst, hot dog, and deli pretzels. By special order, they can buy pretzel numbers and letters, eighteen-inch pretzels, and twelve-inch pretzels. "We've never had it. This is the first time," Malik Jones said as he brought his family in to the main store. Later, as they ate their pretzels in their van in the store's parking lot, they made a decision. "Good. I like it," Jones said. But it's not quite the same as when you buy it from a vendor on the street.

Gus Koebbe Jr.

205

CORKBALL

As with so many stories on the South Side, this one begins at the brewery. Around 1904, employees of Anheuser-Busch decided they needed something to do at lunchtime. So they whittled balls out of the cork bungs that plugged the holes in their beer barrels. They used broom handles for bats and came up with a form of baseball that's still distinctive to St. Louis and the South Side. There's no running, only a pitcher, hitter, and catcher. Fielders are nice additions, but the number of them is optional. The ball looks like a baseball but is only two inches in diameter, or just bigger than a golfball. The bat is thirty-eight inches long and two inches thick, not much larger than the broom handles first used to play the game. The game is still played at places such as Tower Grove Park, Jefferson Barracks, and a field on Walsh Street just east of Ulena Avenue used by the Gateway Corkball Club.

Just before seven on a Wednesday night in June 2010, members of the Gateway Corkball Club gathered in seats behind two pitcher's mounds in the midst of a neatly kept grass field. Four teams of six played, two at each combination of mounds, batter's boxes, and plates. Marty Kirner, a sales representative who lives in St. Louis Hills, was one of those players. His father—city police officer and Alderman Dan Kirner—long played for the club, so Marty joined in college. "With the club, there's several generations," said Marty, who's been playing for twenty-seven years. "My brother and I play. There's a lot of fathers and grandfathers," said Marty, who has been a club batting champion for more than ten years. Mike Moehlenbrock, a great nephew of Dan Kirner, is among Marty's relatives in the Corkball Club. Mike stopped playing baseball in college and started playing corkball when he turned twenty-one.

Jack Buck, no relation to the broadcaster, is among the old timers on the team. "This league actually started in 1929," said Buck, who has been playing for at least forty years. He pitched until about ten years ago and was club pitching champ in 1993. The names of each year's batting, pitching, and catching champs going back to 1930 are listed on plaques on the wall of the group's clubhouse next to the field. The group started using that field in the 1950s.

Today, the team has about seventy-five active members, although some just drink and play cards in the clubhouse. "It's one of those things I just count on doing Wednesdays," said club vice president John Moeser, whose grandfather used to be a member. "I have to explain it to everybody," Moeser said. When they understand the rules, they're hooked, he said. Among those rules: games are five innings long. A swing and a miss on the first strike is an out, as long as the catcher catches it. A called or swinging strike on the second pitch is an out, as long as the catcher holds it. Any third strike is an out. Five balls over the strike zone is a walk. A foul ball is an out. Whether a hit ball is a single, double, or triple depends on how far it goes. A home run is over a building at the edge of the field. If a batter is hit, it's the same as a walk. "If it hits on the edge of a bone, it's ugly," Buck said. There are two ten-week seasons, and the winners of the first half play the winners of the second half. Then there's an all-star game and a tournament involving teams from all over the area around Labor Day.

Corkball isn't as big a game as it once was. After World War II, each of about forty taverns in the city organized enclosed cages to play the game. Outside St. Louis, there are indications it was played in places as far apart as Peoria, Illinois, Jacksonville, Florida, and even Egypt. Possibly, it was spread by servicemen in World War II. According to one story, a sailor was amazed no one on his ship had heard of a corkball. So he asked his mother to send him a corkball and corkball bat so he could show his fellow sailors how to play. Today, those bats and balls are made in China—where else?—for Markwort Sporting Goods Company of St. Louis. The company's corkball logo includes the words "St. Louis's Classic Baseball Game"—to which someone south of Highway 40 would add, "The South Side's Classic Baseball Game."

GUM BALLS ON THE SIDEWALK

On a tree-lined street in the Bevo Mill neighborhood, a couple live a mostly contented life in a frame house with two cats. Not that there's anything unusual about living on a tree-lined street on the South Side. The Forestry Division of the St. Louis Department of Parks, Recreation, and Forestry maintains about eighty thousand trees between sidewalks and curbs. They add beauty to city life, not to mention shade to relieve the hottest August day. But here is where the couple's contented life becomes mostly contented. Two thousand of the city's eighty thousand trees are the dreaded sweet gums, carriers of the cursed sweet gum balls. One of those trees is in front of the couple's house. One is next door. As regular as swallows returning to Capistrano, the dreaded balls start falling in front of the couple's house in the days after Christmas. The fibrous ugly brown balls with lots of spikes on them drop from different trees at different times. But at their house, they first appear as the couple dump the last of the paper from unwrapped gifts in the trash. First one or two, then a dozen. Then mountains of balls ready to turn the ankles of those foolish enough to step on one. If they're raked in the morning before work, more are on the sidewalk after work. If they're not raked for two, three, or more days, they collect, crying out to the neighbors, "These people don't care."

Almost everybody hates sweet gum trees, but South Siders have a particular reason to despise them. By planting them at the curb, the city guaranteed that the gum balls would stand out horribly when they fell on the sidewalk and street. Amazingly, though, one South Sider—Chip Tynan—doesn't mind them. A horticulturist, he manages the Missouri Botanical Garden's horticultural answer service. Every morning from 9 A.M. to noon, master gardeners answer questions on topics like why weeds keep coming back to their lawn to how to make their daisies better. They may even take questions about what to do about their sweet gum trees. Tynan knows it won't make him popular, but he actually loves the trees. "People think I'm nuts when I say that I like sweet gum trees," he said. "Anybody who sees a sweet gum in its autumn color has to be struck by how beautiful the tree is." The tree is seen in sites from Connecticut to southern Illinois to central Florida and northeastern Mexico. It grows big, and it grows fast. With it comes the balls—fruits, really—containing individual capsules of seeds that fall out of the balls. In mid- to late April, small greenish flowers form. By the time the gum balls fall from the tree, the seeds are long gone. Actually, bird-watchers should like them. Songbirds like the seeds. So do goldfinches, housefinches, and purple finches.

First cultivated in 1681, the trees are used commercially for pulp, lumber, and veneer. Missouri Botanical Garden founder Henry Shaw included sweet gums in the list of trees to be planted when he developed Tower Grove Park. At one time people included sweet gums on a list of good street trees. Very few kinds of trees can survive well between streets and sidewalks. Tynan hesitates to criticize the city for planting the trees but agrees the balls pose a problem at those spots. Among those problems are how to dispose of them. It can take years for them to break down in a compost pile. "It's one of the few items that I've ever fed into a chipper shredder and had it emerge out the other end almost intact."

Tynan has heard of people sticking them together with wax for a fire starter. They also make great tabletop Christmas trees. Just put them into a pyramid, stick them together with a glue gun, and spray on white paint to give a frosted effect. Placed on the top of a flowerbed, they can keep away cats and rabbits, or so the story goes. Something called the Nut Wizard is supposedly great for picking up acorns, walnuts, and gum balls without bending over. These can be effective, Tynan said, but added, "People are always looking for a reason not to go out and use a rake." A hormonal spray is said to reduce the number of flowers and thereby the number of balls. But it's nasty on metal paint, especially the finish of your neighbor's BMW, Tynan said. He recommends that professionals do the job. Even then, there's no guarantee the product will work. It has to be applied when the tree is at full bloom. This once caused consternation to a forestry service that was asked to spray four or five trees, each of which bloomed at a different time.

One effective way to get rid of the menace is to chop the trees down. A disadvantage to this solution is that it's illegal without a permit. For what it's worth, the maximum penalty for violating any city ordinance is a mere five hundred dollar fine, court costs, and ninety days in jail. City judges usually don't put people in jail for violating ordinances. Exasperated homeowners might consider it a reasonable expense. However, another disadvantage to this is that a tree chopped down next to a street may land on a neighbor's car. It's possible to avoid most neighbors' cars by performing the chore on street cleaning day, when people are issued tickets for not moving their cars from the street. On the other hand, it's still dangerous. If anyone was stupid enough to do this, the authorities doubtless would get out their law books and find violations that would cost somebody much more than a five hundred dollar fine, court costs, and ninety days in jail. So don't do this. Or don't say where you got the idea.

In the long run, the best way to deal with the mess from sweet gum trees is not to plant them. That's what the city is doing. Although they're good trees for shade, the city's Forestry Division has given up on planting them between sidewalks and streets, Forestry Commissioner Greg Hayes said. But they're still planted in parks. "We get a lot of complaints," Hayes said. The city's pledge not to plant any more sweet gum trees isn't enough for the couple in Bevo Mill who already have two sweet gum trees in front of their house. To them, the trees are part of the passing of the seasons. The balls start to fall after Christmas. The fall continues through the cold and into the start of spring. Then the leaves come out and the falling stops. The leaves provide the front yard with a deep shade into the fall, when they turn golden. Then they fall and are raked away. The tree is barren as Thanksgiving turkey goes on the table and as guests arrive for the couple's early December Christmas party. They mail Christmas letters and buy gifts for relatives in distant cities. Then the day comes, and they open packages they've received from afar. That night, after watching Clarence once again save Jimmy Stewart from making a big mistake, they rest in a satisfied sleep. The next morning, the man heads outside to pick up his paper. On the sidewalk he spies his first gum ball. So ends one passage around the sun. So, on the South Side, begins another.

ACKNOWLEDGMENTS

In this second edition of Hoosiers and Scrubby Dutch, I have a second chance to praise all the people who made this book possible. As with all my books, I must acknowledge the love, encouragement, and helpfulness of my wife, Lorraine, both in this project and in our thirty-four years of marriage. In addition, I must thank the editor of the first edition, Matt Heidenry, and my publisher, Josh Stevens, for allowing me to write for them.

My editors at the *Suburban Journals* deserve thanks for allowing me to report about St. Louis's South Side from 2001 to 2010. During that time I learned about many of the subjects covered in this volume and developed many of the impressions reflected herein. Some topics were also subjects of articles I wrote for the *Journals*. However, in all but a few instances, the research and reporting for the essays in this book are new. The bibliography contains a list of the essays that originally appeared in other forms in the *Journals*, along with the dates of other articles I wrote that I consulted for reference.

Librarians Adele Heagney, Louise Powderly, and Cynthia Millar did a terrific job of finding materials for me at the St. Louis Public Library's Central Branch. So did Ron Bolte and the other volunteers at the Carondelet Historical Society. Others who deserve mention include Charles E. Brown, assistant director of the St. Louis Mercantile Library, the staff of the St. Louis Board of Public Service, Catherine A. Smentkowski, the many who granted me interviews, and others who helped along the way.

Thanks to all who agreed to interviews for the second edition, including Martin Duggan, Mary Tomazi, Guy Slay, Bruce Marren, Mike Algarda, Morton Hill, the grads of St. John the Baptist High School who let me sit in on their luncheon at Bill Gianino's, local Donut Kings, Anthony Duncan, Steve Smith, Sandy Cohen, Brooks Goedeker, the gang at Hodaks, and Neil Svetanics.

Finally, thanks to you, for buying and reading this book and for putting up with my jokes in programs I gave about the first edition. If something you read here adds to your knowledge, makes you think, or brings a smile, I've done my job.

BIBLIOGRAPHY

Two essays in this book are revised versions of articles previously published in the *Suburban Journals*, with additional material added. They are the ones on Chic Young and Betty Grable. They are used by permission.

Several new essays were added to this second edition of *Hoosiers and Scrubby Dutch*. Essays deleted from the first edition can be found at jimmerkel-thewriter.com

Interviews

Mark Abbott, professor of history, Harris-Stowe State University, May 7, 2010.

Mike Algarda, April 28 and April 30, 2014.

Michael Allen, architectural historian, January 19, 2010.

Barbara Anderson, retired volunteer director, St. Louis Psychiatric Rehabilitation Center, April 9, 2010.

Brad Arteaga, photographer, May 4, 2010.

Eldon Arteaga, photographer, May 4, 2010.

Josh Boeks, manager, nine St. Louis recreation centers.

Ron Bolte, president, Carondelet Historical Society, March 20, 2010, and other times.

Charles Boyd, pretzel salesman on Idaho Avenue at Loughborough Avenue.

Pat Brannon, owner, Casa Loma Ballroom, May 29, 2010.

John "Jack" Buck, Brian McCarthy, Marty Kirner, Matt Klein, Mike Moehlenbrock, John Moeser, members, Gateway Corkball Club, June 9, 2010.

Ryan Calaway, Bevo Mill shotgun homeowner, May 23, 2010.

Sandy Cohen, Rick Ruzicka, and Doug Wolf, July 24, 2014, at Globe Drugs, with follow-up conversations.

Andy Colligan, Missouri Botanical Garden archivist.

Bob Corbett, Dogtown resident and historian.

Stephen Conway, Eighth Ward alderman.

Slim and Zella Mae Cox, gospel singers and Chippewa Street furniture dealers.

Anna Crosslin, president and chief executive officer, International Institute, St. Louis, May 5, 2010.

Florence Deppe, Betty Reinbold, and Virginia Palazzolo, residents of the Altenheim, 5408 South Broadway.

Fati Dime, owner, Cisse's Fashion and Hair Braiding Salon, May 6, 2010.

Martin and Mae Duggan, May 14, 2014, with follow-up conversation and correspondence.

Anthony Duncan, May 30, 2014, and follow-up conversations.

Billie Ferguson, owner, Ferguson's Pub, March 7, 2010, along with customers John Dennis, "Brian," and waitress Barb Gannon.

Jennifer Florida, Fifteenth Ward alderwoman, May 2, 2010.

Rita Ford, president, Gravois Park Neighborhood Association, June 5, 2010.

Mickey Garagiola, brother of Joe Garagiola, May 1, 2010.

Brooks Goedeker, June 12, 2014.

Esley Hamilton, preservation historian, St. Louis County Department of Parks and Recreation, January 19, 2010.

Greg Hayes, commissioner, Forestry Division, city of St. Louis.

Morton Hill, July 1, 2014.

Mike Howard, Dolores Morfia, and Billy Watkins, at Five Star Senior Center, June 11, 2010; and Don L. O'Toole Jr., all about Bucket Joe.

Andrea Hunter, tribal history preservation officer, Osage Nation, June 7, 2010.

Ruth Kamphoefner, Lafayette Square pioneer, April 27, 2010.

John Karel, director, Tower Grove Park, April 6, 2010.

Dorothy Kirner, former Twenty-Fifth Ward alderwoman.

Gus Koebbe Jr., owner of Gus' Pretzels.

Katherine Kozemczak, volunteer at Chatillon-DeMenil Mansion, May 29, 2010.

Arlene Kruse, owner, Kruse Gardens, Columbia, Ill.; Evan Ely, Tower Grove South; Scott Androff, photographer; Matt Leitch; and Yolanda Thompson, on May 22, 2010, in Soulard Market.

Sadic Kukic, Bosnian restaurant owner, April 24–25, 2010.

Lance Lindner, September 11, 2014.

Marty and Sue Luepker, owners, Al Smith's Feasting Fox Restaurant, along with customers.

Sue Maehl, former resident of house on top of Sugarloaf Mound, June 7, 2010.

Bruce Marren, nephew of Mickey Garagiola, May 1, 2010, April 26, 2014.

Mickey McTague, numerous interviews.

Gina Meyer, owner of Hill neighborhood shotgun house, May 5, 2010.

Steve Mizerany, appliance dealer, May 24, 2010.

Vince Mizerany, son of Steve Mizerany, May 24, 2010.

Robert Moll, Tower Grove East neighborhood resident.

Bob Morris, friend of Steve Mizerany, May 24, 2010.

Sheryl Myers, July 25, 2014.

John Pearcy, Gary Craig, Don Griffith, Peggy Clanton, Freeman Daigle, Aaron Hines, Kay Schwarz, and Eddie Strickland, April 2014.

Monsignor Sal E. Polizzi, Hill neighborhood community leader during battle to erect the Edwards Street Overpass over Interstate 44, June 8, 2010.

Lewis Reed, Board of Alderman president, May 6, 2010.

Beverly Remspecker Spinner, Patricia O'Shaughnessy Vogel, Katherine Stehlin Dunivin, Ruth Hohmeier, Jeanne Christian Meyer, and Lois Bosch Kennedy, May 23, 2014.

Mark Rice, former volunteer with the Chippewa Street Frog Garden.

Carol Savio, Hill neighborhood real estate agent, May 6, 2010.

Craig Schmid, Twentieth Ward alderman.

James F. Shrewsbury, former Board of Aldermen president.

Dan Sinclair, son of Dave Sinclair, April 7, 2010.

Francis G. Slay, mayor of St. Louis, January 26, 2010.

Guy Slay, July 2014.

Steve Smith, July 18, 2014.

South Siders Mike Carril, Julie McNeal, Norma King, "Glenn" and Van Johnson, asked about definition of "hoosier."

Carol Surgant, daughter of Ruth Kamphoefner, Lafayette Square pioneer.

Neil Svetanics, interview with follow-up questions.

Harry Swanger, Compton Heights neighborhood resident.

Kourtney Thomas, July 22, 2014.

Mary Tomazi, April 29, 2014, April 30, 2014, May 2, 2014.

Kacie Starr Triplett, Sixth Ward alderwoman.

Chip Tynan, manager of the horticulture answer service, Missouri Botanical Garden, May 6, 2010.

Steve Vollenweider, organizer of benefit for American Diabetes Association, May 29, 2010.

Todd Waelterman, St. Louis street commissioner, late April 2010.

Brian Wahby, chairman, St. Louis Democratic Committee.

Fred Wessels, Thirteenth Ward alderman.

Canon Michael K. Wiener, rector, St. Francis de Sales Oratory, May 4, 2010.

Walt, Kim, and Danny Wiseman; Pete, Pat and David Lecko; Marguerite Still; and Melissa Hegerstroem, all interviewed at Ted Drewes, 6726 Chippewa Street, May 15, 2010.

Joseph Winkler, manager, research collections, St. Louis Public Library, July 24, 2010.

Phyllis Young, Seventh Ward alderwoman.

Books

Conley, Timothy G. *Lafayette Square: An Urban Renaissance* (St. Louis: Lafayette Square Press, 1974).

Curzon, Julian, editor and compiler. *The Great Cyclone at St. Louis and East St. Louis, May 27, 1896: Being a Full History of the Most Terrifying and Destructive Tornado in the History of the World* (Carbondale: Southern Illinois University Press, 1997. Originally published by Cyclone Publishing, St. Louis, 1896).

Duggan, Mae and Martin, *Donnybook* (St. Louis: Together Press, 2000).

Faherty, William Barnaby. *Henry Shaw, His Life and Legacies* (Columbia: University of Missouri Press, 1987).

Garagiola, Joe. *Baseball Is a Funny Game* (Philadelphia: Lippincott, 1960).

Griesedieck, Alvin. *The Falstaff Story, Second Edition.* St. Louis, 1952.

Herbst, Henry, Don Roussin, and Kevin Kious. *St. Louis Brews: 200 Years of Brewing in St. Louis, 1809–2009* (St. Louis: Reedy Press, 2009).

Hernon, Peter, and Terry Ganey. *Under the Influence: The Unauthorized Story of the Anheuser-Busch Dynasty* (New York, London, Toronto, Sydney, Tokyo, Singapore: Simon & Schuster, 1991).

Houck, Louis. *A History of Missouri from the Earliest Explorations and Settlements Until the Admission of the State Into the Union, Volume II* (Chicago: R. R. Donnelley & Sons Co., 1908).

Hyde, William, and Howard L. Conard, editors. *Encyclopedia of the History of St. Louis: A Compendium of History and Biography for Ready Reference* (New York: The Southern History Company, 1899).

Jackson, Rex T. *James B. Eads: The Civil War Ironclads and His Mississippi* (Bowie, Md.: Heritage Books, 2004).

Kamphoefner, Ruth. *Lafayette Comes Back* (St. Louis: self-published, 2000).

Koch, A Ryrie. "Carondelet Yesterday and Today." St. Louis: unpublished manuscript, 1933.

Krebs, Roland, in collaboration with Percy J. Orthwein. *Making Friends Is Our Business: 100 Years of Anheuser-Busch* (St. Louis: Anheuser-Busch, 1953).

Lossos, David A. *St. Louis Casa Loma Ballroom* (Charleston S.C.: Arcadia Publishing, 2005).

McAdam, David H. *Tower Grove Park of the City of St. Louis.* Prepared by Oorder of the Board of Commissioners (St. Louis: R. P. Studley & Co., printers, 1883).

Merkel, Jim, *The Making of an Icon: The Dreamers, the Schemers, and the Hard Hats Who Built the Gateway Arch* (St. Louis: Reedy Press, 2014).

O'Connor, Msgr. P. J. *History of Cheltenham and St. James Parish, Commemorating the Diamond Jubilee of St. James Parish and the 25th Anniversary of the Coming to the Parish of Rev. P. J. O'Connor, Pastor* (St. Louis, 1937).

O'Neil, Tim. *Mobs, Mayhem & Murder: Tales from the St. Louis Police Beat* (St. Louis: St. Louis Post-Dispatch Books, 2008).

Plavchan, Ronald Jan. *A History of Anheuser-Busch, 1852–1933* (North Stratford, NH: Ayer Company Publishers, Inc., 1969, 2000. Originally published by Arno Press, 1976).

Rother, Hubert and Charlotte. *Lost Caves of St. Louis: A History of the City's Forgotten Caves* (St. Louis: Virginia Publishing, 1996).

Taylor, Philip. "A Brief Description of Soulard Market, Past and Present: Acquisition of Lands Pertaining to the Property, and Items Concerning the Soulard and Cerre Families." St. Louis: unpublished manuscript, 1975.

Tighe, Betty Konersman, and Ron Bolte, *St. John the Baptist Parish: A Short Story of a Great Catholic Family* (St. Louis: Saint John the Baptist Catholic Church, 2007).

Twain, Mark. *Life on the Mississippi* (New York: Harper, 1951).

Weaver, Dwight. *Missouri Caves in History and Legend* (Columbia: University of Missouri Press, 2008).

Young, James A., and Cheryl G. Young. *Seeds of Woody Plants in North America, Revised and Enlarged Edition* (Portland, Ore.: Dioscorides Press, 2009).

Newspapers and Other Publications

Alton Telegraph, October 17, 2009.

Bugle, December 1, 1979.

McKinley High School *Carnation*, 1915–19.

Missouri Historical Society Bulletin, date unknown.

Missouri Republican, October 1, 1864.

Naborhood Link News, May 9, 1979.

Riverfront Times, February 27, 2002.

Saint James Parish Newsletter, March 30, 1952.

St. Louis Globe-Democrat, Aug. 30, 1870, Jan. 5, 1872, May 28, 1896, June 7, 1902, Aug. 21, 1915, April 24, 1929, April 28, 1929, June 30, 1929, April 5, 1933, April 7, 1933, April 8, 1933, Nov. 26, 1938, Feb. 6, 1939, July 13, 1940, May 27, 1943, March 28, 1946, Aug. 25, 1951, April 25, 1953, April 26, 1953, April 29, 1953, April 30, 1953, May 7, 1953, June 14, 1953, June 26, 1953, Dec. 3, 1953, Jan. 27, 1954, Aug. 8, 1956, Oct. 17, 1957, Oct. 19, 1957, Oct. 22, 1957, Oct. 23, 1957, Oct. 25, 1957, Nov. 6, 1957, Dec. 18, 1957, Dec. 28, 1957, Nov. 20, 1958, Jan. 20, 1959, Feb. 10, 1959, Feb. 11, 1959, Jan. 13, 1960, Jan. 14, 1960, Feb. 14, 1960, April 17, 1960, May 1, 1960, Jan. 8, 1961, Jan. 22, 1961, April 30, 1961, July 24, 1961, Aug. 20, 1961, Nov. 16, 1961, Jan. 15, 1962, June 7, 1962, Jan. 3, 1963, March 22, 1963, July 21–22, 1963, Aug. 24, 1963, Aug. 29, 1963, Sept. 4, 1963, Jan. 28, 1964, April 8, 1964, June 28, 1964, Oct. 1, 1964,

Feb. 24, 1965, April 16, 1965, April 19, 1965, Sept. 29, 1965, Nov. 3, 1965, Dec. 13, 1965, Feb. 18, 1966, May 27, 1966, Sept. 15, 1966, Nov. 6, 1966, Feb 4–5, 1967, Feb. 20, 1967, March 27, 1967, April 16, 1967, May 10, 1967, July 13, 1967, May 3, 1968, July 18, 1968, Sept. 11, 1968, Nov. 26, 1968, Nov. 28, 1968, Dec. 12, 1968, May 19, 1969, June 16, 1969, June 21–22, 1969, June 28–29, 1969, July 19, 1969, Sept. 25, 1969, Dec. 7, 1969, Jan. 16, 1970, March 18, 1970, Jan. 17, 1971, Aug. 27, 1971, June 3, 1975, June 9, 1975, June 13, 1975, Oct. 1, 1975, July 1, 1978, Dec. 10, 1979, Feb. 25, 1980, April 5–6, 1980, May 2, 1980, March 29, 1982, March 30, 1982, , Oct. 13, 1982, Oct. 15, 1982, Jan. 18, 1985, June 17, 1985, Aug. 5, 1986.

St. Louis Magazine, December 2009.

St. Louis Post-Dispatch, Jan. 20, 1898, May 19, 1913, Aug. 21, 1915, Aug. 22, 1915, May 9, 1929, March 11, 1933, April 5, 1933, April 7, 1933, April 8, 1933, March 13, 1937, April 7, 1937, March 6, 1938, Dec. 4, 1938, Dec. 11, 1940, Jan. 5, 1941, March 7, 1945, March 10, 1945, April 4, 1945, Jan. 26, 1947, Dec. 5, 1948, March 12, 1949, April 6, 1949, Jan. 6, 1950, Aug. 24, 1951, Jan. 20, 1959, Jan. 28, 1959, Feb. 10, 1959, Feb. 11, 1959, April 23, 1950, Oct. 8, 1957, Jan. 29, 1958, Dec. 24, 1958, Jan. 14, 1960, Oct. 2, 1960, April 5, 1961, April 30, 1961, Jan. 3, 1962, Jan. 13, 1963, March 10, 1963, July 21, 1963, July 22, 1963, Aug. 4, 1963, March 22, 1964, May 16, 1965, July 13, 1965, July 20, 1965, July 21, 1965, Aug. 1, 1965, April 3, 1966, May 19, 1967, July 9, 1967, April 9, 1968, March 17, 1969, Aug. 16, 1969, Feb. 11, 1970, June 13, 1971, March 21, 1974, June 13, 1975, June 3, 1977, Nov. 2, 1977, July 27, 1979, March 2, 1980, March 14, 1980, Aug. 14, 1980, Sept. 21, 1980, Dec. 23, 1980, March 29, 1982, March 30, 1982, May 26, 1982, March 9, 1983, April 23, 1983, Aug. 17, 1983, Dec. 16, 1983, June 23, 1985, June 24, 1985, June 26, 1985, June 29, 1985, Nov. 5, 1985, Nov. 14, 1985, Nov. 15, 1985, Oct. 9, 1986, May 9, 1988, Jan. 13, 1989, Dec. 22, 1992, Sept. 7, 1993, Jan. 13, 1995, May 5, 1996, Jan. 1, 1997, Feb 28, 1997, May 28, 1998, Sept. 18, 1998, Nov. 8, 1998, Nov. 9, 1998, Nov. 10, 1998, Nov. 11, 1998, Nov. 13, 1998, Nov. 15, 1998, May 13, 1999, May 18, 1999, Aug. 22, 1999, Dec. 30, 1999, Jan. 5, 2000, March 7, 2001, March 21, 2001, May 9, 2002, March 3, 2005, June 2, 2005, Aug. 21, 2012, Dec. 29, 2013.

St. Louis Republic, May 28, 1896, Aug. 21, 1915.

St. Louis Star, March 13, 1933.

St. Louis Star-Times, July 12, 1940, Jan. 7, 1950, Feb. 11, 1950, June 20, 1950.

St. Louis Times, Aug. 9, 1911, Aug. 14, 1911.

South Side Edition Suburban Journals, June 24, 2009.

South Side Journal, July 28, 1948, Jan. 3, 1952, Jan. 18, 1989, Oct. 1989, Aug. 4, 1993, Aug. 11, 1993, Aug. 27, 1993, March 27, 1994, March 15, 1995, April 14, 1996, Feb. 25, 1998, Jan. 9, 2000, Dec, 19, 2001, Dec. 19, 2007, Oct. 8, 2008.

Suburban Journals articles by the author: July 20, 2005, Nov. 28, 2007, March 5, 2008, March 12, 2008, Aug. 20, 2008, Sept. 1, 2008, Oct. 1, 2008, Oct. 22, 2008, Nov. 5, 2008, Dec. 17, 2008, Dec. 31, 2008, Jan. 7, 2009, March 4, 2009, March 25, 2009, April 8, 2009, July 1, 2009, July 10, 2009, Sept. 1, 2009, Sept. 23, 2009, Feb. 23, 2010.

Southwest City Journal, Aug. 29, 1990.

Related Material

Allen, Michael. *A Short History of the City Hospital*, 1995 and 2003.

Baxter, Karen Bode, and Esley Hamilton, architectural historians, and Timothy P. Malone, research associate, National Register of Historic Places Registration Form, Stork Inn, March 30, 2000, https://www.dnr.mo.gov/shpo/nps-nr/00000440.pdf (accessed May 31, 2014).

Blick, Boris, and H. Roger Grant. "French Icarians in St. Louis," *Bulletin*, Missouri Historical Society, October 1973.

Colligan, Andrew, archivist, Missouri Botanical Garden, e-mail to author, July 21, 2010.

"Columnist Jim Fox Dies After Long Career," http://www.stltoday.com/suburban-journals/metro/news/columnist-jim-fox-dies-after-long-career/article_1ab07fd6-c384-59de-8f4c-f359d8de00d4.html (accessed May 9, 2014).

Davis, Mark, Union Pacific spokesman, e-mails to author, May 4, 2010, and June 3, 2010.

"Dawn of a New Day for Grand and Gravois," booklet commemorating the opening of South Side National Bank, January 2, 1929.

Drawings of reconstruction of Oregon Avenue between Potomac and Miami Streets, 1927–28, provided by staff of President's Office, St. Louis Board of Public Service.

Engleman, Glennon, Appellant, v. Ruth M. Engleman; Bill McCarvey; Special Agent Atf; unknown agents, Sgt. John McGrady, St. Louis County Police Department, Appellees, United States Court of Appeals, Eighth Circuit – 663 F.2d 799 Submitted Nov. 4, 1981. Decided Nov. 10, 1981, court papers.

The Great St. Louis Bank Robbery, starring Steve McQueen and directed by Charles Guggenheim, 1959.

Josse, Lynn. Landmarks Association of St. Louis, Inc., National Register of Historic Places, Multiple Property Documentation Form, St. Louis, Missouri, Public Schools of William B. Ittner, 1902–1910.

Josse, Lynn. Landmarks Association of St. Louis, Inc., National Register of Historic Places, Nomination Form for South Side National Bank, March 23, 2000.

"Facts about the Climatron: Missouri Botanical Garden," fact sheet published by the Botanical Garden around the time it opened. Undated.

"A Game Born in St. Louis," *Missouri Historical Society Magazine*, Spring 1999.

"A Historical Look at Al Smith's Feasting Fox" on back of menu, Al Smith's Feasting Fox Historic Restaurant & Pub Banquet Facilities, undated.

"Entertainment Hot Spots Putter Out," by Jim Fox, http://www.stltoday.com/suburban-journals/metro/opinion/fox-tales-entertainment-hotspots-putter-out/article_c0baaef8-d6fc-5914-8405-de21e2b4de2d.html (accessed May 10, 2014).

Feld, Wally, general manager, St. Francis de Sales Oratory, e-mail to author explaining problems with the St. Francis de Sales Church steeple, May 12, 14, 2010.

"Fighting Fires Once Took Real Horsepower," by Jim Fox, http://www.stltoday.com/suburban-journals/metro/news/fox-tales-fighting-fires-once-took-real-horsepower/article_7fa8788a-2b80-54f1-99c0-d794d76ef96a.html (accessed May 9, 2014).

"Fox Tales: Instant Lifestyle Has Its Shortcomings," September 5, 2012, http://www.stltoday.com/suburban-journals/metro/opinion/

fox-tales-instant-lifestyle-has-its-shortcomings/article_b337f04c-1ad7-58af-ad9b-6951ef37a240.html (accessed September 11, 2014).

"Funeral Friday for Jim Fox, Longtime Newspaper Columnist, Who Died at 91," by Tim O'Neil. http://www.stltoday.com/news/local/funeral-friday-for-jim-fox-longtime-newspaper-columnist-who-died/article_617c48d5-c3c4-5aa8-9d3e-696938ff0935.html (accessed May 10, 2014).

Gruntfest, Eve, University of Colorado, and Daniel Pollack, Yeshiva University, "Warnings, Mitigation and Litigation: Lessons for Research from the 1993 Floods," paper, http://opensiuc.lib.siu.edu/cgi/viewcontent.cgi?article=1400&context=jcwre (accessed July 3, 2014).

"Help Restore an Historic Landmark," St. Francis de Sales, http://traditionfortomorrow.com/ (accessed September 11, 2014).

"I'm a True South Sider Through and Through," by Jim Fox, http://www.stltoday.com/suburban-journals/metro/opinion/fox-tales-i-m-true-south-sider-through-and-through/article_7d51f0ea-aa89-5939-b658-93978e4f94a6.html (accessed May 9, 2014).

Jefferson, Albert. *The Negro of Carondelet* (St. Louis: undated).

Kicked Out by an Awkward Clown https://www.youtube.com/watch?v=LuWLMD72YMc (accessed April 29, 2014).

Longwisch, Cynthia H. Landmarks Association of St. Louis, Inc., *The Early Public Schools of William B. Ittner*, St. Louis, 1897–1901, 1990.

"Many South Side Landmarks Nothing But Memories Today," by Jim Fox, http://www.stltoday.com/suburban-journals/metro/opinion/fox-tales-many-south-side-landmarks-nothing-but-memories-today/article_cb1c8bed-c1d1-5567-b768-2768a95a2b20.html (accessed May 10, 2014).

McTague, Mickey, letter to Thomas J. Mullen, Aug. 24, 2001.

Murray, Thomas E. "You $#^%?@ Hoosier!: Derogatory Names and the Derogatory Name in St. Louis, Missouri," cited by Graf in "The Word Hoosier," 1987.

National Register of Historic Places Inventory—Nomination Form for Chatillon-DeMenil House, December 1975.

Official Map of the City of St. Louis as Established by the City Charter of 1876. Prepared under the direction of James W. Suelmann, director of streets, 2001.

Oprah Winfrey Network Fall Sneak Peak: Sweetie Pie's, http://www.oprah.com/own-sweetie-pies/OWN-Fall-Sneak-Peek-Sweetie-Pies (accessed July 9, 2014).

O'Sullivan, Katie, spokeswoman, St. Louis Metropolitian Police, e-mail to author, April 29, 2010.

Polizzi, Sal. E., Monsignor. "The Edwards Street Overpass: A Lesson in Political Expediency." Research paper submitted to the Graduate School of Saint Louis University in partial fulfillment of the requirements for the degree of master of arts in urban affairs, 1972.

Rehkopf, Susan, e-mail to Theresa K.M. Danieley, forwarded to Jim Merkel, Jan. 27, 2010.

Roussin, Donald L. Jr., e-mail to Matthew Heidenry, July 21, 2010.

Rother, Charlotte and Hubert E. "Historic Caves of St. Louis, Mo.", *Missouri Speleology,* Vol. II, No. 3, July 1970.

Schmid, Craig. *Explanation of Vote Regarding Floor Substitute for Board Bill No. 122 According to Rule 47 of the St. Louis Board of Aldermen*, letter inserted into minutes of Dec. 11, 2001, Board of Aldermen meeting, printed in Dec. 26, 2001, issue of the *City Journal.*

Schottzie's Bar and Grill menu, http://www.schottzies.com/menu.html (accessed September 11, 2014).

"St. John the Baptist School Must Raise $250,000 or Face Closure," http://www.stltoday.com/news/local/education/st-john-the-baptist-school-must-raise-or-face-closure/article_529a30c3-9c09-58d6-b326-e01944b938ac.html (accessed July 6, 2014).

St. Louis City Directory on microfilm, 1917, 1951, 1952.

St. Louis City Directory on microfilm, Polk, 1969.

St. Louis Ordinance 36527, approved January 31, 1928.

St. Louis City Revised Code Division 1: Traffic Code.

Stan Kann with Bill Cosby, https://www.youtube.com/watch?v=AbPuC2-IJJ4 (accessed July 1, 2014).

"Stores Once Nickel-and-Dimed Way to Success," by Jim Fox, http://www.stltoday.com/suburban-journals/metro/opinion/fox-tales-stores-once-nickel-and-dimed-way-to-success/article_78e72c53-472f-54c1-90f3-d968e14deef0.html (accessed May 10, 2014).

"Two South St. Louis Catholic Schools to Close," http://www.stltoday.com/news/local/metro/two-south-st-louis-catholic-schools-to-close/article_e87fddf6-febd-57f9-83c6-b3b828dbf263.html (accessed May 24, 2014).

Undated news release from Rawlings Sporting Goods Company containing reprinted material on corkball history and rules, from *Rawlings Roundup*, Volume 1954, No. 4.

"World Wide Magazine at the St. Louis State Hospital," https://www.youtube.com/watch?v=7h0OPP2LoxQ (accessed April 29, 2014).

"World Wide Magazine—the Preposterous Perusing Perspectives of Pete Parisi," https://www.youtube.com/watch?v=EZK5bCHuvds (accessed April 29, 2014).

Websites

American Experience: "Secrets of a Master Builder: How James Eads Tamed the Mighty Mississippi," http://www.pbs.org/wgbh/amex/eads.

Anheuser-Busch, "Beer Is Back," http://www.anheuser-busch.com/press/beerIsBack.html.

Corbett, Bob, page on Icarians, http://www.webster.edu/~corbetre/dogtown/icarian/icarian.html.

Corbett, Bob, page on Dogtown, http://www.webster.edu/~corbetre/dogtown/dogtown.html.

Desco Group website, Hampton Village Plaza, http://www.descogroup.com/Property_Detail.aspx?propid=341 (accessed July 1, 2014).

Excerpts from "A Walk Around the Square" by Thomas Keay, http://lafayettesqr.com/neighorhood/Shared%20Documents/History.aspx

Fabulous Fox website, http://www.fabulousfox.com/stankann.aspx (accessed July 1, 2014).

Facebook page about Bucket Joe by southcitystl.com website, http://www.facebook.com/topic.php?uid=2207600760&topic=7879.

fox2now.com/2013/04/07/races-held-saturday-for-the-young-and-young-at-heart/ (accessed May 2, 2014).

Globe Drugs website, http://globedrugstl.com/ (accessed July 26, 2014).

Gooey Butter Cake: Gooey Butter Cake History and Recipe, copyright 2004 by Linda Stradley, http://whatscookingamerica.net/History/Cakes/GooeyButterCake.htm.

Graf, Jeffrey, "The Word *Hoosier*," Reference Department, Herman B. Wells Library, Indiana University–Bloomington http://www.indiana.edu/~librcsd/internet/extra/hoosier.html.

International Institute of St. Louis, www.iistl.org.

Lindner's Pub website, http://lindnerspub.webs.com/, (accessed September 11, 2014).

National Weather Service page on major St. Louis tornadoes, http://www.crh.noaa.gov/lsx/climate/torcli/city.php.

Neighborhood Histories by Norbury L. Wayman published in 1978, St. Louis City website, https://stlouis-mo.gov/government/departments/planning/cultural-resources/neighborhood-histories.cfm (accessed July 1, 2014).

Osage Nation, video recorded during an all employee meeting on August 18, 2009, at the Wah-Zha-Zhi Cultural Center. Sugarloaf Mound and its relation to the Osage Nation was discussed by tribal history preservation officer Dr. Andrea Hunter of the Ozark Nation Historic Preservation Office, http://www.osagetribe.com/executive/welcome_sub_page.aspx?subpage_id=54.

Osage Nation, "Sugarloaf Nation Comes Home," news release, July 31, 2009, http://www.osagetribe.com/executive/news_story.aspx?news_id=1522.

River des Peres Watershed Coalition: Introduction–River Timeline, http://www.thegreencenter.org/rdp/introduction/timeline.asp.

1916 River des Peres Plan in St. Louis, Summary of Historic Planning Documents, http://stlouis.missouri.org/government/duffy/riverfront.htm.

Schmidt, Louis, "The Confederate Raid in Dogtown on September 29, 1864," http://www.websteruniv.edu/~corbetre/dogtown/history/schmidt/schmidt3.html.

Soulard Market, http://stlouis.missouri.org/citygov/soulardmarket.

St. Francis de Sales Oratory, http://www.institute-christ-king.org/stlouis.

St. Louis Business Journal, "City Hospital Transformed into The Georgian Condominiums," October 13, 2004, http://stlouis.bizjournals.com/stlouis/stories/2004/10/11/daily48.html.

St. Louis movie theaters, http_movie-theater.org_usa_mo_stlouis_MO St. Louis.PDF (accessed May 18, 2014).

St. Louis Psychiatric Rehabilitation Center history page, http://dmh.mo.gov/slprc/history.htm.

St. Louis Public Library, The Naked Truth page, http://exhibits.slpl.org/germanamerican/data/SiteDetail240012748.asp.

St. Louis Street Index, St. Louis Public Library website, http://www.slpl.lib.mo.us/libsrc/streets.htm (accessed mid-July, 2014).

thegrovestl.com (accessed July 9, 2014).

Ted Drewes, http://www.teddrewes.com.